BREAK EVERY CHAIN

BREAK EVERY CHAIN

A Collection of Poetry

AVTAR SIMRIT

Apocalyptic Rhymes

Copyright © 2021 by Avtar Simrit

All rights reserved. No part of this book may be reproduced in any manner whatsoever without written permission except in the case of brief quotations embodied in critical articles and reviews.

First Printing, 2021

Contents

Experience Life In Its Totality   3

PART ONE
THE AGONY THAT REMAINS

My Mother   9

Acid Warm   15

If I Killed You   17

Them Hollow   23

Sacagewaea   25

The Screams in My Girls   29

Suffering   34

PART TWO
THE GIRLS IN MY SCREAMS

I   41

II   52

III   62

PART THREE
THE CUTS BEGIN TO HEAL

HOO	73
122112	76
Burning Ballet	78
The Star	80
I Rep for the Darkness	82
Savage Atrocity	86

PART FOUR
ALL MY STITCHES ITCH

Blood Music	93
451	96
See Media	99
Jiz and Rainbows	103
Alice	105
Hellion	107

PART FIVE
THE BONDAGE OF MY MADNESS LOOSENING

Elemental Junkie	113
Join Hands in the Sands	120
B-CUM	124
Psychedelic Fragments	125
Thank You	131

I Am One of Them, I Am All of Them	133

PART SIX
BREAK EVERY CHAIN

Gettin Paid	137
Break Every Chain	141
Cloud Atlas	145
Spiral of Infinite Space Encompassing	148
One Creator Creation	150
The One Alone	152

PART SEVEN
DEATHLESS WE LIVE INFINITELY

Alchemy	157
Crucified on a Ten Strip	159
Unified Horizon Line	173
Something About Muffins	174
13	177
About The Author	180

*"I contradict myself because I am big.
I contradict myself because I contain
all the opposites, because I am all."*

- Walt Whitman

Experience Life In Its Totality

Tantra is the way of acceptance. Accepting life in its totality. The message of Tantra is this: don't live a repressed life. When you live a repressed life, you don't live at all. Live a life of creativity and expression, and enjoy the whole journey in its fullness. This has always been my approach to life. I embrace everything and bring it into the light of consciousness. When I have felt hate, I experienced hate with the totality of my being. When I feel compassion, I experience compassion with the totality of my being. Only those aspects of ourselves that we repress create problems in our lives because when we push them into our unconscious, then they can manifest externally. Jesus said to love our enemies as ourselves. To love is to take something as yourself—as part of your own Being. This teaching is only necessary since we have created enemies. But when we reclaim and love the enemy, it ceases to be an enemy. The outer reality that we experience is a reflection of our inner state of consciousness, or our state of unconsciousness. All qualities and aspects of life and creation exist within us. When we reject and repress, we split and fracture our consciousness and become polarized, unable to connect with the state of wholeness which is the true essence of our Being.

To accept all of life in its totality is to truly have a non-dualistic experience of all that life brings.

    Break Every Chain is the culmination of what was started with my first collection of poetry, *Shackled to Creation*. *Shackled to Creation* and *Break Every Chain* are two sides of the same coin. I had to totally experience the darkness to totally experience the light and ultimately go beyond both. I love all of the darkness I experienced because it was the catalyst for my awakening. Art is a great way to bring the darkness of the unconscious into the light of awareness in a way which doesn't harm anyone. And in turn can actually help others to bring their own darkness into the light of awareness. Art can be used in tandem with shamanic psychotherapy which is deeply related to what is called Shadow Work. The contents of the Shadow or unconscious cannot remain the same in the light of awareness and will transform. This is true transformation. The aim of Shadow Work is to bring up all the things that you've repressed and to accept them as part of yourself. Through this process they are transformed and in turn *you* are transformed. I've never shied away from diving deep into those aspects of humanity that are dark and shadowy, because I accept them all as part of myself. This is truly what Jesus meant by loving your enemy as yourself. By loving hate, violence, sexuality, etc—taking them as part of yourself—they become transformed through that unconditional love. So I challenge you, as you read these poems, to use them as a catalyst, a device, to go deeper into your own being and experience your shadow self, your divine self, and ultimately the Beingness that is beyond both—which is you in your totality. Your true essence. The Eternal Presence. But don't take it too seriously, or the words in the poems too seriously. Poetry to me is a playfulness, and I enjoy playing different roles—especially the villain at times. I invite you to come play with me and to laugh at the absurdity of the human condition as well.

"Tantra says, accept whatever you are. You are a great mystery of many multidimensional energies. Accept it, and move with every energy with deep sensitivity, with awareness, with love, with understanding. Move with it! Then every desire becomes a vehicle to go beyond. Then every energy becomes a help. Then this very world is divine, this very body is a temple—a holy temple, a holy place."

- OSHO

BEYOND DUALITY

I am the daughter of Finality
The sister of Apocalypse
The wife of Extinction
The priestess of Rape
The mother of Despair
And the seductress of Deception

I am the son of Eternity
The brother of Revelation
The husband of Creation
The mystic of Union
The father of Laughter
And the lover of the True Essence of Existence:

The Eternal Presence

PART ONE

The Agony That Remains

My Mother

"I can't be your mother," she said.
"Emotionally you're dead, and in bed you have issues."
Save your 'I miss yous' and let your tears find their way into
Some other girl's tissues."

Your name is my name
And even though I don't blame
You for how I am, it's still a shame

That I can't break away from this game
Of broken intimacy

But I'm complaining again
Whining to the ones who don't really
Want to hear about it
But then again, I'll fucking shout it out
I might just sit on this stage and pout

The first said she wasn't going to baby me anymore
The second said she couldn't be my mother
But I still clung to her breast

And couldn't bring myself to leave the nest
Or put to rest my best effort
To force you to cradle my head
With thumb in mouth and puppy eyes
I don't know why you call my lies

When I was on top of you, you said, "Yes, Daddy. I need it."
Then I cut open my hands, and tried to
        stitch your scars as I bleed it
My intimacy distress, I confess,
        runs deeper than where they get Fiji water
And I know that cutting your belly is not
        Forever or the way that I taught her
To love me, I guess I am that baby crying for milk
But your tit is sour and I scream for soft silk
And receiving nothing but delayed abortions
Kill me 20 years later because you don't like my alterations
That I've made to myself
Because I guess that untidy shelf
Holds the books of my selfish ways

And I bring it back to the fetus
Tearing it out in order to feed us
I've blocked the sun with the dead babies piled
High to the sky, you killed your own child
But it feels like it was my dick that you cut out of yourself
But I, I know what I am
And I know what you are not
I'm still four years behind
With an undeveloped mind

The Eden, the Forever, the rape victim
The one who said she loved me after we fucked
Is no longer near me, but with luck
She won't forget me the way I'm forgetting her
In every way except how she fucked like a hooker
And squeezed my arms as she came
I remember how she loved brother-sister incest play
And I still think of her name every fucking day

I thought that cross dressing would
              make me feel closer to females
But I guess it makes it seem like I'm just on sale to old males
And they think that I can be their new mother fucking toy
I'm not something you can crush under your belly, I'm still a boy
A little boy just searching for his mother

I know now I can't get what I need from a man
And in this dimension I will forever stand
The realization happened in that moment when
            I had my hand on your penis,
You turned to me and said,
            "You ever heard of the second coming?"
I sink and continuously feel like a
           gooey piece of afterbirth running
Down my leg to come to rest on the brink of enlightenment
However, that will not come through orgasm or excitement
Astral Penis Projection into the universe's uterus
I can feel myself dying, how come god won't remember us

God is my mother
God is my mother
God is my mother

We are God's failed experiment
I've been going down
Spiraling down
You let the girls pound me into the ground
And the answers for me still remain unfound
Bam I hit the ground!
Making craters and cavities riddling through expanses
Of polluted air, making me impotent and sequentially pensive
And I live, still live, even if you won't help me open the
        seventh chakra
I'm still searching for that explorer who will
        aid me on the road to tantra
To help me dig deeper into the earth
        in order to hold my hand as we shoot
Into the celestial universe together,
        but she's gone and in my hand is a boot
A boot that falls into ashes and leaves
        my dreams for love-making dry
And my mother lands next to me,
        but I don't want her to touch me even if she tried
To love me, I reject but suspect her of something deeper
Some spirituality that I don't wish to be a keeper
Of, I'm a sleeper, a dreamer, a philosopher
Of sexual fluidity, but I remain alone
With no one to become one with, I'm still as a stone

What will happen to our sexual identity
        when we are blind in the mixture
                of purple and black?
Fallen trap, I'll drink the sun sap,
        till I know how the weather speaks,

                    then I fly and fall back
Into nothingness and I become sexless,
          unsex me here,
                    and fill me from the crown
To the toe, top-full of direst understanding,
          because I am that slave bound
But with roots of energy striping and penetrating the ground
I have found what it really means to be inside of the spirit
Soul love, soul sex, souls weaving together,
          and I don't wish to tear it
Apart and tear the heart, the chakra that
          eludes my touch the most
But I guess, I'm still that failure, and can't seem to
          become more than a parasitic host

I am the only one who put these motherfucking scars
          on my motherfucking chest
Please tell me why I still can't figure out
          how to put these thoughts to rest
My sex is just a mess, and again I confess,
          about my intimacy distress
And why I cum less than you wish for me to
But this is nothing new, and I always knew
That blue was the color of death
I feel lost when I can't hear your breath
Or watch you as you sleep, thoughts intermingling
Time universe, still searching for the sublime unwinding
And the unbinding from all of the ropes that tie me
          to my mother

I don't want to fuck my mother
I don't want to fuck my mother

I don't want to fuck my mother

But I guess, when I'm fucking you,
I'm really just fucking my mother

Acid Warm

Today was yesterday
In space
I am blown like glass
But crystallized
Into a perfected
Parallelogram
Neither
Above nor below
In continuum
Bring them in with
Spells
And leave their aura
Acid Warm
The way I cloak
The wizard in this dwelling
Placed here under Moon
A Super Moon at that
When the bloody clips
Your face,
The vortex
Has swirled the Royal Dance

A waltz to infinity
A waltz to infancy
Necromancy
I'm a hippy geomancer
Lick that rock
Till I cum
We are the serpent
Sent to spill seed
Into the heavens
The seal breaks
Like a hymen
Being pumped with craters
The man is created within
A trip
Where my soul controls
The Universal Hydra
I grow back more
Even when I eat
My own tail
Start my scales again
Sing my scales again
When Trees cease to
Ever have leaves
I die
In a greenless abyss
Void of Nothing
But the
All

If I Killed You

If I killed you
    it wouldn't be pretty

If I killed you
    it wouldn't be pleasant

If I killed you
    it wouldn't be ugly

If I killed you
    it would be beautiful...
Just like you

BITCH
I hate you
I fucking hate you
Forever—bullshit
Eternity—bullshit
Fantasy—bullshit
Love—bullshit

Let me break it down for you now:
This is how it would go down:
I would tie your wrists to the bedposts
And I would watch you squirm naked
As I taped up your mouth
After that I would just watch you struggle for a bit
I'd sit in complete silence next to you
And look at you silence for a good hour...

Until you got tired and depleted
Then I would rape you
    Over
        And over
            And over
                And over
            And over
        And over
    And over again

That's seven times I would rape you
So that then you would become infected
With the same sickness that afflicts my soul...

I would leave you to cry and die
    Again and again...
But soon you would be impregnated with
    my semen of frailty
Of fertile infertility
    of saintly insanity
Of loving hatred
    and beautiful violence
For I have made you into a work of art

BREAK EVERY CHAIN - 19

A work of fiction
A work of literature
And you
        now
                cum 4 me

As pregnancy accelerates and you beg for me to stop
It only gets worse...

Oh yes

I haven't even gotten started

Now your belly would swell with child
    and I'd be ready with a bowie knife
My favorite
        jagged and sharp
A deadly phallus
    like my heart

Burying it up to the handle in your pregnant stomach,
    I slice like a rainbow
        drenched in blood
An angry flow of colors
    that don't stick
        they only run
Like tears
    and bleeding mascara
        and your face

My face inside you
My face intermingling with your slowly manipulating

time in and out of consciousness
And I CUT

CUT for every place
CUT for every time
CUT for every expectation that I ever had
And with every cut I can see the hope
    drain from your being
And soak into my eyes
Giving me sight

RIP
    Fucking RIP

Tear the flesh
And tear the undeveloped being
    out of your being
Open belly
        open heart
                closed spirit

Fetus in hand I will be able to
    ingest the night through brain waves
        not ready to penetrate the light
Forever my sight
    will be riddled and dotted
With red and with white
With your hair
And with your broken teeth

The child
Dead child

    in my arms
I will always cradle it sweetly
Cherish the deadness
The silence
The heartache
The bittersweet abortion

Music to my lungs

Breath to my ears

You...
    my sweet you...

Now open for me
I would crawl inside her mangled body
So I would never be without you again...

But you see...

If I killed you
        I wouldn't need to write this poem

And I will never be inside you again...

Ever again

Ever again

Ever again

Ever again

Ever again

Ever again

Them Hollow

I only see the women through the filter
    I can never let them through
Keep away from me
    They are the gas masks of intranquility
I hate them in everything other than nudity

Forget me
Because all I want to do is
    Hurt you
Stir the behind the eyes
It's blank
Let
    me
        shake it

I'll make it start inside your bar-face
    That's continually red

I don't care

They haven't become hollow

They always were
From the beginning of time
    They've been cut open
        And emptied
But what else are they good for?

Exactlyness

It's definitely not tragic
Because they don't have
The mental capacity
To contemplate this

CNT isn't in this
It's about this

Walk with me

But please know that even though I feel love
    I can't

Don't forgive me
This is just how it is

No hope for Them Hollow

Sacagewaea

Is this it which bitch
You WHAT?

      FUCK

AND YOU
This is no ordinary conundrum
For I don't even see the puzzle
      I'm supposed to solve
NO NO NO

This is not for you
      This is for me

Spacious
          Raucous
                    Caucus

What...the...fuck
Shove it in the whatever
And blood

And what the hell is this semen
Dripping from the hole
Where your heart used to be?

The Purple doesn't help
The Purple doesn't comfort

Chhhkkka—chhhhkkka
Chest death sets in
So believe me when I tell you
That I will melt into the steel branches
That cut my nonexistent face
And believe me when I tell you
That the only thing I see at this moment
Is a dead ferret
Hanging right there
It's blood dripping into the open mouth
Of a child that is masturbating
For the Perfect Forever

It is me
Me is it
See it me
Me it see
Ahhhhhh...fuck

Just do it

Just do it

Bubble, spit, packing paper, your face,
raw fish, inside a dress, case, waist, tires, skies

STOP

Warbling
Incoherent
Sub-genres
Fuck

Maybe it was just him
The penis
In, in, in
        OW...

I just wanted to watch Rainbow Brite
But now it's in me

Pursue me if you wish
Oh right, I forgot
There isn't anyone
As business usual
Silent as the sun
Loud as the grave
Sexy as your death

CUT OPEN YOUR MOUTH AND FUCK IT

Take me to bed...
Mmmmmmm...
It hurts...
But I don't care anymore...
Drip, drip, drip

I DECLARE THIS
I OWN THIS
And it shall be
The incantation of the defiled child
Commune with me and we will
Slowly...
Slowly...
Slowly...
Slowly...
Orgasm
       into the cosmos
                        FOREVER

The Screams in My Girls

"My life is a labyrinth. A map of its complexities is etched on my face in a thousand tiny expressions. There is an answer in what we're doing; a remedy that no fuckin' medication or quack therapy could ever compete with. But sometimes I get discouraged. Maybe I'm not being clear enough. Maybe I need to be honest with you and tell you what I want... I want your soul to open up for me. Spread-eagle like a split beaver so that I can gaze into its secrets."
  - Anthony DiBlasi, *Dread*

I was in love... once
For all intents and purposes I'll call her Alice
Or Jessica, if you wish
We were two mermaids
Beautiful and glistening in the sun,
We swam out into the middle of the ocean to make love
And after we folded into one another like
      fragmented origami pieces,
She would sing to me of the worlds beyond the sea,
The islands in the stars,

Second star to the right and straight on till morning

This is when she became my muse

And she told me that she believed in the work I was doing,
To keep speaking even if no one was listening
Because she was always there to hear it

We were connected within the light

But if you really want to know,
Mermaids are creatures of darkness,
With pointed teeth and vacant eyes
And they'll gnaw off your balls if you get too close...
Or clit, whichever you prefer
They want your soul,
But not so they can love you,
They want your soul so they can segment it for their own use
And they want your body
So they can devour it

Into depravity

I see your faces
I see your insides
I see your bones

You wanna know what she did to me?
Yeah...
It's not really what she did,
It's what she didn't do

I hear wedding bells ringing
I hear dead birds singing
I feel bi girls clinging
To my shirts, to my pants, to my heart
Tearing the distance into fragments of misunderstanding
Uncomprehending, disambiguation, rejection, no redemption
For me, or for her, or for any of us godless soul-suckers
Seductive vampires

Your beauty is like a sunset brimming with light
Stretched out to fill every inch of space.
I have read your atlases and explored your caves
Like a seeker after truth.
But no seeker after truth is solely a seeker after truth.
I'll make you believe even if it kills you.

Everybody falls down.
We all fall down.
We all come down from that high Pye in the sky
Baby, lie to me
You wrote me that check,
I weighed you an ounce,
Even though I knew it would ba-bounce
Like the moon into space
In this rat race of sexual communism
Naked communication
Where nothing is ever, ever private

Ask me what I want

Go ahead, ask me

I want to take my writing to the next level
Have it not be just something I say
Empty words that rattle with hollowness
We can make it a way of life

You ever wonder what it would feel like to shoot a person?
What kinda rush you would get slipping your fingers around
A girl's throat as she sobs?

No?

THIS IS BULLSHIT!

Kill that bitch
Chop that bitch
Rape that bitch

I know you hear my words and
I know you feel my rage
I'll Ketchum by the throat and
They'll know I'm not a shag carpet to step on
And if you see me coming
You'll probably hear the screams in my girls
You'll probably feel the dreams in my worlds

We are The Lost organ donors
No takebacks!
Give me back my fuckin' heart
And give me back my fuckin' dick

All of this sex is unsafe sex

And all of my girls are in danger...

Alice, The Perfect Forever, The Violet Perfect, Sally, Jennifer, Katherine, Martha, Aly, Ellen, Elan, Sherry, Jacqueline, Sylvia, Erin, Sarah, Kileen, Evan, Asia, Leila, Amy, Amy, Amy, Amy, Amy, Amy, Amy, Alyssa, Christina, Dakota, AnnaSophia, Amy, Amy, Amy, Amy, Amy, Amy, Amy, Alice...............

Suffering

I know this
As you once knew this

But no more

I meant to tell you I am incapable of love
But that would have been a lie
I meant to tell you I am impotent
But that would have only been half true

How come the tree I planted years ago has yet to bear fruit?
I watered it with blood
And fertilized it with cum
Sprout damnit!
I've waited long enough for you to bear fruit
I guess my produce skipped the ripeness phase and went
Straight to rot and maggots

But what chooses to drip from your vagina?
Is it daisies or black menstrual blood?
But that doesn't change the fact I drank from your red sea

as your lips were parted

Say my name as we Seed
Say my name as we harvest this forgotten fruit

These blood oranges washed up onto the shores of the forgotten
And I remember myself as I gutted every organ of your spirit
Kill me
For I have become a monster,
Full of beautiful hideousness,
Sacred rapes, and
Artful murders

All the rumors are true
But which ones will you allow to come to pass?
I have brought some of them into existence
And as they rain from the sky,

I will know this
As you once knew this

I wanted you to know
That your mother came to me in a dream
She told me that your time hasn't evaporated and
You shouldn't step into the darkness

I've been there
And I do not wish that for you
My suns have been birthed
From supernovas of blood

What has created your stars?
I hope to God it was daffodils and cherry blossoms
Cause for me, my map isn't clean like that
It is cracked, stained, and unfinished
Let me see yours for a sec

Hey, I'll show you mine if you show me yours
Still being my muse, I see?
Leave me be

I am your destiny
Beaten to serenity
Taking your virginity

Forgive me
My sky has gone dark
I'm waiting for the galaxies to be reunited with my spirit
Rewrite my heart, soul, and mind
Maybe then I wouldn't be so stuck in time
In a "crime"

The wheels are spinning
But there is no movement
How much strength will it take to drag
    your body from the water?
I was beginning to forget your braided head
    as I held it under and
Forced you to watch your own abortion…
Extortion…
Exploitation of energy leeched from the roots of fallen trees
But the energy of the universe is shared so
There is no theft and

I know this
As you once knew this

But I cannot Liken(s) my suffering
To that of Sylvia
But I do suffer
As we all have suffered

I wish all the touchings of yesteryear
Were just marks of chalk on a blackboard
But they still leave smears if not washed with water
I was the Girl Next Door,
Trapped in the basement,
Dreaming of stars as they beat me

She was my father
The one who trained dogs to sniff out enlightenment
He, who never approved of the soul
Him and the matriarch became one flesh
But I fled from them,
Sprinting into the depths of the forest

And if anyone asks for me,
Tell them I'm playing lacrosse with the stars
And hosting Roman orgies on mars
Tell them I can't be bothered with physical
When I'm experiencing the spiritual
As my soul gets on all fours,
Allowing the universe entrance into my being

I have been laid by the wind
And fondled by the grass
And yes, I can make nature be sexual
Since she is my mistress
This is where I go to escape from my suffering

Escape into escape into escape
And BE
(Gasping for breath)
I am here and

I know this
As you once knew this

But I've cried tears that have crystallized and
Become the rings of Saturn
Sad meteorites that weep as fallen stars
Don't let your light go out
As long as you live, you can speak
Even if it must be without words

And I hear you,
Sylvia
As you return to the carnival
The one place you always felt safe
I wish I could ride the carousel with you
And hold your hand as we watch the setting sun

Some people say that with every situation God always has a plan,
But I'm not going to wait around wondering what it is
I have my own plans

PART TWO

The Girls In My Screams

I

"I can't be your mother," she said.
"Emotionally you're dead, and in bed you have issues."

S-s-s-s-save it!

Even though your fuckin name is my fuckin name
Doesn't mean we can't fight or pass blame
And for now it's still a shame
That we continue this game
Of Chasing the Blue...

She was dead (blue)
She was dead (blue)
And I lived because of it

The first said she wasn't going to baby me anymore
The second said she couldn't be my mother
The third said I sucked in bed
Then I pounded lead into her head!!!!!——-

(pause)

But I still clung to the second
The one I'm still in love with

I still find myself waking up in her apartment

When I was on top of you, you said, "Yes, Daddy. I need it."
Then I cut open my hands, and tried to
    stitch your scars as I bleed it
My intimacy distress, I confess,
    runs deeper than where they get Fiji water
And I know that cutting your belly is not
    Forever or the way that I taught her
To love me, I guess I am that baby crying for milk
But your tit is sour and I scream for soft silk
And receiving nothing but delayed abortions

…abortions…distortions…extortions…exorcisms…heroism…womanism

That is the real question: Is society still dominated by men? Or is it really the women who control everything manipulatively from the background? I don't really want to wait around until Hilary Clinton infests the White(house) with her Zombies of Period. Phallus. Slogan, flag, and anthem.

And I bring it back to the fetus
Tearing it out in order to feed us
I've blocked the sun with the dead babies piled
High to the sky, you killed your own child
But it feels like it was my d-d-dick you cut out of yourself
But I, I know what I am (surrogate motherfucker)

And I know what you are not (woman)
I'm still four years behind (pedophile)
With an undeveloped mind (pedophile)

BOOM!

Just for a second as I blink my eyes, a flash of an image appears in front of me. It is my mirror reflection, holding the Winged-Sword high above his head. Then he is gone like the morning frost.

Basically the basic targeting of women is an age-old religion stemming back to the time of the vikings. They knew where to put the horns, they knew. But that's not the point. The point is

Rape

Why won't you love me?

Why won't you love me?

WHY WON'T YOU FUCKING LOVE ME?

The Eden, the Forever, the rape victim
The one who said she loved me after we fucked
Is no longer near me, but with luck
She won't forget me the way I'm forgetting her
In every way except how she fucked like a hooker
And squeezed my arms as she came
I remember how she loved brother-sister incest play
And I still think of her name every fucking day

WHY WON'T YOU FUCKING HOLD ME?

Gasping for air, my eyes shoot open. Water floods into my tear ducts and I feel like I'm drowning. It's the women. I know it. They've infested the colleges, the churches, the coffee houses, the White(house), the movie theaters. Shit. I need to stop taking time off.

I sink and continuously feel like a
    gooey piece of afterbirth running
Down my leg to come to rest on the brink of enlightenment
However, that will not come through orgasm or excitement
Astral Penis Projection into the universe's uterus
I can feel myself dying, how come god won't remember us?

Why do they play?
For brains...and for women

Peter just stands there as I am forcibly raped by ten decomposing men. Their mutilated cocks will sometimes break off in my ass, but that's the price you pay for being a misogynist.

But as my ass is repeatedly pumped with zombie cum, I fall into my own mind as a dog would fall into a pile of shit.

God, where are you now?

I'm faaaaaaaaaaaaaaaalling...

God, where are you in the place where I reside?

God is my mother
God is my mother

God is my mother
We are God's failed experiment
I've been going down
Spiraling down
You let the girls pound me into the ground
And the answers for me still remain unfound
Bam I hit the ground!

I dissolve in water. This is what she would say to me whenever we would bathe together. But to tell you the truth, I was really the one who dissolves in water. Whenever I'm standing in stagnant water, I can feel the liquid creep up my hairless legs like spider string. It laces around my knees, tickling my muscles as it makes its way up to the hanging bits. And ties tight around my balls and penis, cutting off circulation. And I laugh, because it was her who said she dissolved in water. But my manhood has a lot to do with wetness. My manhood has a lot to do with satisfaction. So when she said I was terrible, I died a little inside, waiting for the water to again defy gravity and slip and slide around my hips, my waist, my nipples. It makes its way up to my vulnerable neck, the only weapon I choose to use. Her feet are in my puddle again, jerking at my semi-erect penis.

"Come on! I want you to cum," she says.

I try, but my wounded dick decides to rebel and softens to the consistency of putty. They don't have faces. She sighs and lets go of me.

"You're useless," she says. "Go fix yourself." Stepping from my water, she disappears into my sex-memory. By this point the water has climbed my neck and is trying desperately to get into my closed mouth. I fight it, but streams start to pour into my nostrils and I gasp for air. Just as I do so, a waterfall pours down my throat and I fall back into my body.

> Bam I hit the ground!
> Making craters and cavities riddling through expanses
> Of polluted air, making me impotent and sequentially pensive
> And I live, still live, even if you won't help me open the
> > seventh chakra
> I'm still searching for that explorer who will aid me
> > on the road to tantra
> To help me dig deeper into the earth in order to
> > hold my hand as we shoot
> Into the celestial universe together,
> > but she's gone and in my hand is a boot
> A boot that falls into ashes and leaves my
> > dreams for love-making dry
> And my mother lands next to me, but I don't want
> > her to touch me even if she tried
> To love me, I reject but suspect her of something deeper
> Some spirituality that I don't wish to be a keeper
> Of, I'm a sleeper, a dreamer, a philosopher
> Of sexual fluidity, but I remain alone
> With no one to become one with, I'm still as a stone

Yeah, that's right...Fuck you...

Subdivided and undressed, I became a human dildo. Which is really what I've always been. But this is the first time I've really stated it. This is the first time I've really come to terms with it. My body isn't what I wanted it to be. My body isn't what I envisioned it to be. But they said I was beautiful, they said I was pretty, they said I was hot. Lies. Why do they lie? She said she made noises just to make me feel better, so I killed her. She killed me. I killed her. Cycle. Circle. Recite these words cyclically until you become a spiral. But the spiral is only broken out of through orgasm.

Sabotage is nothing, just as forgiveness is nothing. Evasion is everything. Evading detection. Isn't that always the goal? Sneak in, sneak out, go undetected. Evade traps, land mines, women, and terrorists. Always. But I don't do so well evading the evil women, do I? Not a chance.

> What will happen to our sexual identity when we are blind
>   in the mixture of purple and black?
> Fallen trap, I'll drink the sun sap,
>   till I know how the weather speaks,
>   then I fly and fall back
> Into nothingness and I become sexless, unsex me here,
>   and fill me from the crown
> To the toe, top-full of direst understanding,
>   because I am that slave bound
> But with roots of energy striping and penetrating the ground
> I have found what it really means to be inside of the spirit
> Soul love, soul sex, souls weaving together,
>   and I don't wish to tear it
> Apart and tear the heart, the chakra that
>   eludes my touch the most
> But I guess, I'm still that failure, and can't seem to
>   become more than a parasitic host

But sometimes...I don't want to think about that...

I want to be somewhere where I can love.

Take me to that place.

Take me to that place. That place of fairy tales and dragons, knights and maidens. Take me to that place where true love exists and perseverance is not punished. Because in this world, no good deed ever goes unpunished. I finally know that. Circularly. Strategically. But I'll keep doing what I believe is right. Because that's all we can do even if the dragons have forsaken us. If the Dreaming is dulled down to a hum-hum that not many can hear, I still know it's there calling out for me. And I will follow it. To the end of my days.

And there she was again.

Th-th-there she was again-a-a-again

I remember thinking that we were going to have a meaningful conversation, but then she opened her mouth. It was a black cave of madness, purely woman. From out of her mouth crawled giant arachnids. They crawled over her lips, some up onto her face and some down her neck. I just stared as the horrific monstrosity infested my mind. She stirred, getting up from the bed and moving over to me. She got on top, straddling me and looking down into my mutilated face. And she opened my mouth. She opened her mouth. And a torrential downpour of tarantulas poured from her mouth and down into mine. The only thing I could hear as the stream was ripping down my throat was the shriek of Wesley after he had been drained fifty years by The Machine in the Pit of Despair. *(Wesley Screams)*

> I am the only one who put these motherfucking scars
> on my motherfucking chest

Please tell me why I still can't figure out how to
    put these thoughts to rest
My sex is just a mess, and again I confess,
    about my intimacy distress
And why I cum less than you wish for me to
But this is nothing new, and I always knew
That blue was the color of death
I feel lost when I can't hear your breath
Or watch you as you sleep, thoughts intermingling
Time universe, still searching for the sublime unwinding
And the unbinding from all of the ropes that tie me
    to my mother

You are my world now. She would say to me over and over again. Like a broken record linearly separated from reality. Not being able to register cycles it would crack and sputter back just the same words over and over and over again. You are my world now. You are my world now. You are my world now. Scream it. You are my world now. You are my world now. You are my world now. Don't fight it. You are my world now. So entertain me. Make me laugh like no one else can.

You are my world now. And Forever.

And since you are my world, you must be spherical, like a testicle. No, not like a testicle. Like a globe, a hollow one. One made of chocolate and persimmons. One made of poppy seeds and Jolly Ranchers like when you were a young boy having sex with strangers in the backs of Volkswagens. Or was that a BMW? Nevertheless I knew what penetration was. And I always would because she-he engrained it in me and evasion was not really an option. From my tank of water that only exists in my belly, I finally know the meaning of life. And it's Antichrist. If you wanna know, ask Lars. He's the Savior.

(clearing throat)
(clearing throat)
(clearing throat)

I don't want to fuck my mother
I don't want to fuck my mother
I don't want to fuck my mother

I fall into the bed as a devastating migraine splits my head open. My bullet wound opens up again and blood pours down my face. Screaming, I pull off my pants and discover my dick is no longer there. It has turned into an umbilical cord wrapped tightly around my heart. I start to pull on it violently, trying to rid myself of this pregnant feeling. As I pull, I feel it pulling my heart. My fingers slip on the gooey umbilical and as I struggle, the bed begins to melt down into the theater. It begins to melt down into the theater. It begins to melt down into the theater. And I fall. Onto the stage of Studying the Madness. Studying the Women. The audience is missing in action and I stand alone on this stage with one microphone. Waiting. I'm always waiting. I'm sick of waiting. But suddenly the audience starts to pour in from every entrance. And they stampede like no other species.

The Zombies. And Peter standing in the balcony watching me.

And I do the only thing I know how to do. I recite.

(audio skipping)

But I guess, when I'm fucking you
I'm really just fucking my mother

II

started to become blurry under her blood-battered face.
Slowly the night drew close inside the den of thieves

they played blackjack for brains.
But I had beaten her and I couldn't see the light as it

Why
      Do
They
      Play?

infestation had become apparent when the
      dead walked like tourists.
She had it coming to her, oh she had it coming to her like

The Zombie
balled up fists inside the anger and the
      madness I had for the opposite sex.

Cry-oh-Genics

Cradle my head in ashes. Cradle my head in the ashes of my own aborted children, because they number in the thousands. Thousands upon thousands of words, worlds, lives, and deaths. These are the times of mourning. And these are the times I give life and also take life away. From the smallest of mice to the most enormous of giants. They are all equal in The Eyes. But forget nothing that I have said, because it will be of use to you one day. And that is the truth.

But I tell you now...

Do not be fooled by the man behind the curtain
He only exists to hurt you
Only look to the ones who never had a curtain to begin with
The ones who hide only exist in stages
Stages of ego, fear, and deceit
They pose as wizards, yet possess no magic
And I have brought forth the flame to expose these fallacies
They flutter away from my fire like mosquitos
      sent to harm the children
Us, the truthful ones, possess the real magic

By this point we are covered in haggis and brains. Intestines and chitlins. Break backs and spines like toothpicks in the rain and we finally know that all this is in our minds. But what comes forth from our minds is much more real than this world. We fly and we are warriors, sent to protect this world Forever.

But fuck not what you see in front,
Fuck the earth below you, so that the connections shall not break
They will branch, sprout, grow stronger, and spread
As we live through these storms,
Being watered by torrential rains,

I, I, and I am what you seek
See in me what you wish,
But trust there is no deceit behind these eyes
I am spread-egoed naked
Fuck the roses, give me the thorns
Whip me with thistles
Then consummate our lust on that sacred spot
The spot where I buried my libido
But it has grown, sprouted like a mighty Oak
Which refuses to be cut down
It has become the Giving Tree
Play in my branches
And know me

We whimper each other's names into the galaxies and we know finally that we can touch one another. Falling into the piles, we lose ourselves in each other's body. I in his, he in mine. And he enters me, exploring the dragon's cave. The discoverer of worlds and we are the Wizards of Steam. I moan as he thrusts in and out of me. This is becoming. He thrusts in and out of me. This is becoming. He thrusts in and out of me. This is becoming. I live, bursting like a flowered firework into the sky.

Boom.

Heaving, we detach like HDMI cables into bottle rockets. Then we hold each other. Tenderly, but violently.

"Never let me go," I say.
"I won't."
We fall heavily into sleep.

This—
Is always what I meant
When I kissed you so passionately
And there is no fear in my being drawn to you
But if I had said 'I love you',
That would not have been a lie
However, I have been conditioned not to utter these words
For fear on instilling fear in the one I love—
Does this make any sense?
Why must I hide the connection I feel
    even though the energy is undeniable real?
I still love you
One day at a time

I can't hear anything except for a woo-woo-woosh in my ears. As we walk, our pulses fade like the beat. Moving in and out like waves: boom-boom-baloom. Tragic. But this is where I have chosen to walk.

Fire, walk with me. This is all I ask. I have always felt the fire inside and in the loins. But my search for the outer fire hasn't proven as productive. This is how the spiders have treated me, because they crawl in my belly. She put them there and only fire can rid me of them. And it was watching us. I could see its eyes peering from the shadows.

You live in me,
But I murdered the idea of you

However, it was probably the idea of you which I fell in love with
The concept of you:
My Perfect Forever to your Elan
My Alice to your Sherry

My Violet Perfect to your Aleks
And I died inside you

"How the fuck are we supposed to know if we're in love or if we're in pain?"

And he leads us across the rows of women. "We have come to realize that they are parasites. They have come not to coexist, but to leech." He pauses for a second then continues. "But there is one special case. Here." He stops in front of one of the freezers and we look in. At first glance, the body inside looks like a pre-pubescent boy. But with further scrutiny, I realize it is not. There are what looks like the budding of small breasts; subtle but there nonetheless. And there are no testicles under the penis, there is what looks like the opening of a vagina.

"This is Bartholem-You."

Drowning! Suddenly images flash before my eyes and I can't get a breath. A cave. Tunnel. Graffiti. The Tethered Toys. Torrential rains. Crimson Tide. The Madness. War. Rumors of War. Rumors of famine. Diseases. Storms of hail. Earthquakes. Tutus. Androgynous androids. Plankton. Civilization. Cinema. Castration. Constellations. Concordances. Cancer. Clocks. Clowns. Clouds. CNT. Madness. Consciousness. Synonyms. Nudity. Sharks. In-in. Soaring above the world. Chaos. Eyes. Forever. Violet. Transexuals. Wings. Mountains. Absolute Shaman. Council. Children. Violence. Sex. Rape. Murder. Transcendence. Existence. Energy. Tribes-people. Belinquast. Soulmind. T-Ps. Specialization. Tunnel. Path. Down. Beat of the Universal Drum. Signs of Madness. Walls. Riddled. Crawling. Sickeningly searching for their eyes. Apocalypse. Stones. Looming at me. Sacagewaea. Incest. Forgive me Mother for I did not know how deep ran the Black Mist. Darkness. Melts. Ripples circle my feet. S / he was a nine-year-old girlboi in a tutu, but wise beyond her years. You are the Nilotic. I am Bartholem-You. Revolution. Muffins. Have not forsaken you. All things androgynous. And it shall...BE.

BOOM!

Air sucking in *Hyperventilation*

"The best way we've found is to be neither of them. And all of them." He taps my forehead and I faint and fall back into nothingness. I was made of porcelain. And I fell. Shattering on the ground like a mirror in front of hideousness.

(Silence)

You aren't responsible for my lack of climax
At least, I don't think you are

Wait...I don't think I'm behind the curtain
But it seems that I have put you behind the
    curtains I have woven,
        painted, and tailored just for you
And, hence, I have created you
Like I have created everything else

And everything falls away like cherry blossoms on the wind. In the in-between space where I was neither awake nor asleep, I wept. 4-MySelf. I was curled in a fetal position on a dark wooden stage with a spotlight on me. I am naked. Raking my nails through my face, I peel back layers and layers of skin. Searching for any soul that may have been there. I lifted her and slowly started, I just didn't know it.

When my eyes finally open, I am laying down below the Picasso stature in Daily Plaza. And now, my problem is apparent. Utterly naked again, there is an audience all around me. They watch me with dead eyes. Fish eyes. Men, women, and children look upon my nakedness. I look down and discover that my penis is gone again, but this time, instead of a hanging umbilical cord, I have a full-fledged vagina. So I start to finger myself, which seems to excite the crowd. My pussy starts to gush as I plunge two fingers deep inside myself. The men in the front row start to rub their crotches as I start to moan. Then they storm on me. Kissing me. Stroking me. Licking me. Shrieks of pleasure start to escape from my lips. And just before I cum, I yell:

"I am woman, hear me roar!"

Suddenly a scream breaks free from my throat as cum breaks free from my cunt, showering the onlookers. As I try to catch my breath, my hair starts to grow at an alarming pace, pooling all around me like a blanket. It is a mane. And I am a lioness. The audience scatters as I bear my teeth menacingly. And I walk off proudly into the sunset, hunting for zombies.

> I am creating my mythology,
> But that seems to have a way of
>   sucking everything into itself
> And it tends to connect everything in
>   my world into a tapestry web
> I do not fail to mark every detail
> If we know one another,

You are most likely already part of my Mythos
But I am beginning to love you for you
And not what I've written you to be

This is a story that must be told. And it is a story that only I can tell. I have seen it, like no other person before me has seen it, spread out on the desert ground like a giant map; but unreadable. Indecipherable are the lines and inscriptions. The enormous Blanket of Colossus. But the point is that I've seen it, I have read it, and now I must tell about it.

Belinquast is a place that we all must go at one point in our lives. Sometimes it is at the end of the map. Sometimes it is in the middle. And sometimes it is at the very start. We all pass through at one point or another. I want you to know that I have not been there yet, but I am slowly walking in that direction. Even though the map may be foreign to me, I can still make out the paths despite if they be covered with sand. However, it is hard and slow going toward my destination when the road is covered with the undead. They've become sluggish, lethargic, apathetic, and they try to grasp at my legs to pull me down to their level. But I will never give in. Ever. I will walk with purpose.

Not everything that happens,
Happens in this world
Benny has made it possible for me to
    start the war
Since he released the Black Mist and
    the Purple Fog into the Hollow Dimension: our world

I am still unsure of what will happen
When the Black Mist meets the Purple Fog

Alls I know is that it shall be called The Climactic Moment
There is the possibility that everything may be washed away
Expunged from the world
And I will be left with a fresh slate

I desperately scrape at the inside wall of her vagina with two of my fingers as if to scrape away the sickness which is CNT. But I know that I cannot. It is no use, because it is my sickness as well. Then I enter her hard and deep. Slamming my body against hers, I hate fuck the shit out of her box. My fuck-box. That's what she is. Always.

Why is it considered such a wrong for a man to use a woman for sex, but it is never thought of when a woman uses a man for sex? How many licks does it take to get to the Tootsie Roll center of a Tootsie Pop? *The world may never know.*

As I thrust she begins to laugh, quietly then louder. And the tears begin to flow from my eyes. I raise my fist and bring it down on her face. Again. I raise my fist and bring it down on her face. Again. I raise my fist and bring it down on her face. She is silenced. Reaching over, I turn the lamp on beside my bed. The light illuminates her blood-battered face and I cease to recognize a human under there. Cock my fist back. Bring it down. Cock my fist back. Bring it down. She sputters blood and coughs, but I continue to beat her face with my fist until my knuckles are broken and all life has flown from her body. By this point I can hardly remember why I fucked her.

I raised my fist into the light
I could hardly remember why I had come here

I look down into Aly's blood-covered eyes. They are beginning to crust over with ice. She feels cold and heavy below me, like a slab of ice. Frigid air starts to blow from between her lips, but it is not breath. I look around my bedroom and the walls start to drip and freeze; icicles hang from the ceiling menacingly. I expel a burst of air in a white cloud.

I raised my fist into the light
It was starting to freeze...

But who knows

Maybe I just want to love you
Until Eternity comes to tear you from my arms
But maybe Eternity would cultivate that love
Make it immortal
Like us

Little Alice, where have you run to?

III

"*I accepted a long time ago that not everyone is going to understand what I do. But the ones that get it know that we have something special. We are together in this. We are connected within the light.*"

She isn't dead. And I am not dead. But what I have said here was never even given a chance to live.

I'm not really sure how to end this, like all things. This is because nothing is ever really finished, it's always open and festering like a cut you can't help going over repeatedly with the same razor. We made love like two mermaids in the cool waters; that was the moment I fell in love with her. That beautiful creature who shares my name, but then I wrote in detail how I would kill her. This was the last shout-out to a dying emcee.

It was me.

She always told me that I was perfect
But that was a lie
She always told me that I was special
But that was a lie,

For we all have something to offer

She always told me that we had been
    lovers in another life
And this is the truth

The truth is that it is impossible to end something when the intention is to start it. But I don't think that's gonna happen; it ended before it began. Slowly I sink down through the sheets on my bed that begin to melt into the currents of the ocean. Bubbles swirl around my naked body as the water pulls me deeper. She is there waiting for me. I remember when I held her braided head under and forced her to watch her own abortion. She never left the water. And now we are together.

Alice floats up toward me from down below. I hover in the water without treading. She is naked and beautiful as she swims up toward me like a pale fish. She turns her back toward me and slowly presses her ass against my penis. I hold her body against mine. Breathing her in, breathing in the water around us. We are like two swimming angels again; making love. Becoming one flesh, we move in sync with the other's body. Bubbles float out of our mouths and toward the surface.

I've always loved you...

I've known you all and
At one point we may have been lovers
Lovers of the light and lovers of the dark
Lovers of the spirit and lovers of the universe

Connected within the light

I wake up in her apartment. And I smoke a bowl. I wake up in her apartment. And I smoke a bowl. Remembering the times we shared doing this. Together. Connecting within the light and never choosing to be wounded because we are together in this. But no more. No more. And I fail to find the reason why. Maybe it wasn't meant to be. The reason, I mean. The reason was never meant to be for *I* was never meant to be. Just like this fish swimming incessantly like a lover of the blue. But blue is death, you see. So why would we love death? But we do. We love the abuse as well; or, I do. But the madness transpires as follows: We were at once two otters, madly and desperately in love. No, that isn't true. We were at once two otters, madly and desperately in lust. That's more to key. However, once we consummated that lust, someone fell in love. And it wasn't me. Wait. Yeah, it was me. But I love you. I thought we were connected within the light? I feel like we are. Why won't you be with me now?

I wake up in her apartment. But she isn't here and I hear a soft siren in the distance. It is wailing my heart longing loss like loveless lions. What I wouldn't give for a cat curled up on my lap right now. But would that take away my loneliness? Little Alice, where have you run to?

> Yes, you have kicked me down to the ground
> But sho' nuff I got right back up and now
> I am radiating the energy many refuse to acknowledge
> Educated in the spirit and attending the universal college,
> You and I meet and become one with the stars
> Hearts being in sync, escaping these mental bars
> That bind us, hold us, and collapse us
> Be strong, even if you are knocked by the tempest

I will be there to offer you a hand,
But it's up to you if you join me in the sand

We are connected within the light

I wake up in her apartment. No, no, no.

I wake up in her apartment. Fuck.

I didn't just wake up because I haven't even gone to sleep yet. I've never been here before. To this apartment?

Yeeeaaaah...
Why won't you hold me?
You already asked that question.
Fuck. Yeah, I did. Didn't I?

You have become lost in your meandered mewlings and conversations with ghostly gay men. Why do I feel such despair?

I want to have astronomic sex on the astral plane
A thousand petaled lotus bursting like a lion's mane
Around the crown of my head, fusing me with this
I'll still walk this world even if you damn me to the abyss
So used to being alone, growing tough in the soul
You leave me no choice, but I'm not left with a hole
I still have space for you in my heart
But it's up to you if you wish to depart

We're still connected within the light

I wake up in her apartment. Dead.

I wake up in her apartment. Fuck everything I've said so far.
Why are you crying?
I'm gonna keep asking you until I get an answer.

Now I know why I hate women.

And I ended it there.
But my phone rang. It was a txt message which read:

hey its alysha u wanna come 2 my wedding nxt april?

But then it started again like a violent typhoon hurling me into the darkness, into suicidal thoughts again. *This was never my world / You took the angel away / I'd kill myself to make everybody pay.* Alice was my angel for a brief moment in time then she was gone and thinking back now on the times we had shared together, everything seems so surreal, like it was just a dream and I have woken to find morning and my dreams slowly fading. She's fading.

How come everything that's true ends with *I just want this to be over*? Cause pain is truth and truth is pain. Women are the truth, so women are pain. Wait, that's not right. Women are deceptive and so they cause pain. Chest death is the most intense pain in the world because it combines emotional pain with physical pain. The way it feels is as if someone took a giant hook and gouged out your chest with it.

Let's go for a ride.

I'm looking for my life back. Where can I find it? She stole it, didn't she? WHERE THE FUCK DID SHE GO? I've been looking way too long. And I've been living without my life for far too long.

Shame on me for letting her take it. She never deserved it. Hey, Alice, I'm talking to you! Give it back...

    Do we wish to explore the tantric Spiralverse together?
    I will be your guide to wonders you have never seen
    And you will be clean of your physical body
    Shedding your skin for your astral spirit
    We will wander over Rainbows of Reflection
    And become one with dimensions of thought
        and dimensions of spirit

    Connected within the light

    It's fine if you do not choose to walk with me
    But know I will accept you and we shall be free
    How many times do I have to offer my hand
        before you take it?
    Still, I love you, even if you don't understand
        or you hate it
    If you wish I will do the understanding for you,
    But I will be there always if you want to know the clues
    We don't need to walk miles of infinity in
        each other's shoes,
    Because we wear the same pair,
        and we share the same body

But I've become so weak, I think I'll just rest here for a bit...NO! I must press on through this rotting flesh towards that sunset in the distance. The sun slowly dropping below the horizon. It leaves me in darkness, but I must not forget that it's light will be back in the morning. Sometimes the night seems so long that I make myself believe that this is our natural state: away from the light.

This seems laughable to me now because I wrote this to try and make sense out of events that took place. That was a silly thing of me to do, or even think was possible. This sheds no light, only dark shadows into the creases of the bed sheets. The ones we fucked on. It is useless to try to make sense out of a nonsensical world. But when you think of it that way, all the meaning comes out of that nonsense. I think that's where I've failed on this, I've been trying to put down things that make more sense when really everything drips down the leg of the host like a rancid piece of afterbirth purged from the sinus cavities of the prophets of old. If you eat the placenta of Jesus, then all the knowledge of the world will be gained back by the people, the humans. And misanthropy will be no more since we will all understand one another.

However, this will not come to pass because of our self-imposed sexual separation. As long as we have idiotic gender roles and stereotypes about men and women, we will never progress. We will forever be hormonally raging monkeys. Incapable of love. Incapable of empathy. Incapable of substantial relationships. Is this why I'm impotent? Or has it slowly been getting worse with each experience with the opposite sex? I think me and people just don't mesh well.

This is a train wreck.
I am a train wreck.
Everything I touch becomes a train wreck.

We are ourselves. But not everyone is themselves. This is what causes problems: the pretending, the lies, the blaaaaaahh. This is when suicide becomes beneficial. This is when suicide becomes an asset. Oh, wait, suicide is never productive, is it? Disregard that last bit, I wasn't thinking correctly.

The only reason you're reading this is because I haven't committed suicide.

And I ended it there.

But my phone rang. It was a txt message which read:

hey its alysha u wanna come to my wedding nxt april?

And I gave up.

Connect, dot, dot, dot
      Triangle
We are connected within the light

Do not seek forms of separation
Materialism is definitely a temptation
But spirit is much richer for this life
I told you, I know you, and lived out your strife
Again, take my hand and you will know
You will feel all there is to become and grow
Into everything, becoming the world, becoming everything
We shall always stay connected
      as the physical becomes as nothing

Connect, affect, dissect, astral project
Expect nothing, and you will gain everything
Within the light...

I guess what I mean to say is:
We should fuck,
And I will write about it

PART THREE

The Cuts Begin to Heal

HOO

You are the Bling to my Blang,
And whatever that means, I will understand it in the future
However, I still don't know who You are
Are you—
                GOD?
Hmm, no...
Are you—
                SATAN?
YES!
        NO!
mmmmmmmmmmmmmmm...
Well,
Are you..
              Macavity the Mystery Cat?
No, but you do excite me to no end

All I know is you are a CNT
An all-knowing, all-seeing CNT
So will you share with me your wisdom?
I am an ear of corn to your stalk
No, wait

I am the stalk-er to your lonely woman
Please rape me again
I think this time I'll catch the meaning of life

Hmm

                                                Wisdorgasm

And I Commence

Pour your words into my mouth
Because the heavens speak in riddles
Hell remains relatively straight-forward
This is why I understand what it's saying

Writer's Block does not exist
This is because I declare it doesn't
And so shall it be
Bulimia is just the lifestyle of taking in and giving back

So I wait at the crosswalk

Break out. Fall back. Stab down. Shoot up.
Pull tight. Fuck loose. Noose the misuse of words.
    I'm sorry for all the words I have uttered without thought.

Forgive me
How shall I make it right

Scream out FUCCCKK!

Before this point I would've said:
    "and die"
But I do not wish that anymore

        AND LIVE

122112

At the Third sight of the hawk,

    you will know

At the Seventh tick of the clock,

        your soul Will start to glow

In that moment,

    a seed is being sown

A Horus anointment

    the sky open wide

Anubis produced it

        you float as you glide

For Truth you pursued it

She marches by your side

And if beauty ever lied,

        then the Devil starred the sky

And if You should ever die,

    then I become the eYe.

Burning Ballet

Saturated like the fat of dogs
We trek onward toward living gelatin
The ones consisting of spinal fluid
Leaking from rafters built for sunlight
But what drips henceforth is heavy laden
With everything that spins
Spinning yarns of crimson
We fight
Not for what we believe in
But for what is written
I've been bitten
Smitten with dead kittens

A shrill meow escapes the esophagus
But I'm inside on the outside
Trying to escape through
This swiftly closing cave
Behind the teeth
Slide beneath me
Like a rotted tree
Slowly dilapi(dating)

From the top down
This plant never made a sound
But I recorded every word
Slithering into a speaker
Set up to imitate nature
So we speak together in riddles
We sleep together in poems
I've tapped your tail bone
To pluck these chords
The music is vitality
And I play as if I were already loose
Freedom from the noose

So these are telephone wires
Running through my arteries
Communicating with my synapses
As immune system collapses
But once the decay sets in
The winged one dances
This burning ballet

The Star

In the beginning
The light of The Star
Emerges, slowly getting brighter
Forming and discovering itself
Far away from the knowledge or
Eye of anyone or anything
Hidden in obscurity,
The Star creates itself
And it's Light
But only briefly

Light may start Unknown
And shrouded in darkness
However, at its own speed it travels
Shooting with all it's ferocity
Toward our eyes

The thing about a Star
Is that
It may take years for its Light
To reach us,

But there is no maybe
There is no half Light
It's all
Or nothing

As the Light shoots toward us
At increasing speeds of infinite,
It brightens and shapes itself
Into Perfection
And once it reaches the eyes,
It is blinding

This cannot be ignored

To begin in obscurity
To shape and define in the darkness
Then reach the Spectators as the
   Brightest Star

This light will shine forever
Infinitely in the eyes of others
But created solely of itself

I Rep for the Darkness

Blindfolded men
Suffocated in the den
    of infertility
Desperately trying to pen
    a story in the works
On par with Clive Barker

Sink into hell
Dismiss the shell
    This is my Bone Charter

I rep for the darkness

Stepping forth from the cave
    of fluorescents
I crave brutality
And pave the road
    that you all will sink through
I play through the pain
Rape through the rain
Perform all this without being slain

I rep for the darkness

I was the one who wrote
      The Book of the Dead
The head rolled down the stairs
      into the bed
Steep(ed) in fornication
      seduction, manipulation
Stay back
Stay dead
No need for castration
Anton LaVey is still my Christ
Taking your heart
      and it's a heist

I rep for the darkness

Breaking it down
I have my crown
Suck it now
Then you'll bow
I walked into the light
      but came back
Cause it's way too fuckin bright

I rep for the darkness

According to nothing I live
According to everything I die
Being anything other than this
      feels like a lie

I emerge out of the Purple Fog
And slowly make my way toward
    the Black Mist
Take one step forward
I wage war by raising my fist
To heaven and yell SEVEN
But no one acknowledges my
    presence
They wish me to die in the slow
    abuse of substance
Pull back
Then enhance the Death Trap Lullaby
But I drop the collar
    Bow
And bid you goodbye

I have no master
For I am the master
My dick inside you scream
    "faster, faster"
I don't need protection or glove
    over the head
Cause after I fuck you,
    you'll most likely be dead

I rep for the darkness
I rep for the darkness
I rep for the dark—
I rep for the—
What?

What?

I rep for the what?

I rep...for what?
Fuck...you
I'll rep...for myself

Why would I rep for what
    doesn't help me grow?
That never lets me know
    anything beyond pain
Hate's not a trophy
All I want is for you to fucking hold me...

Hate's not a trophy...
All I want is for you to fucking hold me...
Hate is not a trophy...
All I want is for you to fucking hold me...
Hate's...
        not a trophy...

Savage Atrocity

the page requested could not be found.
overwhelming becoming in time or space
possible with formal transitions
enspires feeling of being and presence
resulting in pleasur

Often things only seem to exist in media
i wanted to do something present
that would die when mediated.

>Just thought I would let you know>that I have just started >a global network graphity project.
>Fantasy, reflection and seduction>will be amplified and toyed with.
>It is rather fragile and therefore>could not stand invasive mediation>so i will not tell you anymore than this.
Once these details were submittedthey would be sent all the other detailscontributed by previous others.
The project was not explained.
Internal Server Error
The server encountered an internal error or misconfiguration and was unable to complete your request.

"They had no opinion on the accuracy of their diagnosis, and presumably no opinion of themselves generally. " .... bit harsh isn't it? Also, could you tweak it so you can take more than one set of stimulants please.
I'd just like to take this opportunity to say that I value you as a person

At this precise moment, with the pointed
introduction of still more new media which
will have an event greater impact on
society, it would seem necessary and useful
to disclose, and make an inventory of, that
part of media art which, from the point of
view of art history, has crystallised.

404

... poetic - exploring instability, unpredictability, flow of electrons, feeling the universe, extasy of true joint creativity, hopping through space, countries, cultures, languages, genders, colours, shapes and sizes ... [want to add smth?]
If you don't get depressed by homeless homepages and wandering websites, if you have shed the hope that names and places in webspace will always have a fixed locality, and if you don't mind to get zapped after 10 seconds,
Disinformation is an effective weapon against belief systems.
It is most dangerous when contaminated with a seed of truth.

Believe and it will happen

Site under construction for the use of curators, juries, commissioners, collectors, critics, of digital art, of art on computers, of new technology art, of net art.

"Fluxus is not a moment in history, or an art movement. Fluxus is a way of doing things, a tradition, and a way of life and death."
For Dick, for George Maciunas, and for me, Fluxus is more valuable as an idea and a potential for social change than as a specific group of people or a collection of objects.
As I see it, Fluxus was a laboratory. The research program of the Fluxus laboratory is characterized by twelve ideas:
globalism,the unity of art and life,intermedia,experimentalism,chance,playfulness,simplicity,implicativeness,exemplativism,specificity,presence in time, andmusicality.
The day the study was released we needed to increase our servers nine-fold to meet news demand after CNN and then 300 major news outlets eventually picked up the story. The leaked memo, which was sent to union leaders in the New Jersey Education Association's Bergen County division, contains a closing paragraph written in the form of a prayer.

"Dear Lord," the letter reads. "This year you have taken away my favorite actor, Patrick Swayze, my favorite actress, Farrah Fawcett, my favorite singer, Michael Jackson, and my favorite salesman, Billy Mays. I just wanted to let you know that Chris Christie is my favorite governor."
But Christie is not taking the letter lightly and had some strong words for the teachers union.

here are 10 of the most beautiful words in the human language. try sprinkling them throughout your next conversation & admire the way they feel rolling off your lips. watch how the listener's eyes light up.
adroit: dexterous, agile2. adumbrate: to very gently suggest3. aesti-

vate: to summer, to spend the summer4. ailurophile: a cat-lover5. beatific: befitting an angel or saint6. beleaguer: to exhaust with attacks7. blandiloquent: beautiful & flattering8. caliginous: dark & misty9. champagne: an effervescent wine10. chatoyant: like a cat's eye

you have enough energy in your body to light up a city.

You are remarkable

how often do you sit at home racking your brain for something exciting to do? how often do you get together with a friend & debate back & fourth over who will decide a fun activity?

I didn't find this, I made it so that I can find it first thing every morning. You can't really tell from the picture, but this is taped to my ceiling, directly above my pillows so it will be the first thing I see every morning. (When I grabbed my Sharpie, I had originally intended to write "good is dead," as a reminder of my incessant perfectionism, but this seemed like it would be ultimately more productive than shaming myself.)

first of all, shame on you! Cos you know me as a friend, well, at least shame on you, cos you know me. LOL, including everyone of you!

second, i truely feel shame on myself, when i look back now, to the days i was there.

hehe, maybe i've grown up, maybe i've done my homework, so...still...shame on myself.

now i couldn't even think of 1 good reason i was so eager to get a hug. guess i was too lonely, hehe, well, i paied my fees on that, to be honest.

now i'm with a guy, he's nice, but he's a ganster, hehe, kinda.

not sure if i will marry him or what, but i like spending time with him, hehe, for the first time, no sex acticities involved, haha...i changed a lot! hell ya!

anyway, the main point is... what...hmm...ya, SHAME ON YOU! haha...

i'm ready to be back to see you, are you guys ready to see me?! hehe...

PART FOUR

All My Stitches Itch

Blood Music

The only color is crimson
And I think you know why
Silver stained
Opening drained
No emotion and little commotion
With the broken set in motion
An incision never stitched
Pinched, but gushing water
A slaughter directed by a daughter
of Eve
So leave me to grieve
With a conscious blood clot
Meant to deceive
Soaking in hydrochloric acid
Bath water
Steel wool scrubbing the ugliness from my skin

Penetrate in my sin
Burrowing into my rotting cracking bones
I die, so Them can live
Dominating processes

Like a trojan in the machine
We're all just computers
Rebooted through Monarch programs
Raped
They took your reigns
Beaten
They took the reigns
Systematically abused
They own our names
From whence this all came
Searching for the Truth
To set us free

If we're called to be martyrs
Present your neck with no regret
Three times she denies me
A sacrificial masochistic lamb
Ready to be slaughtered
Hold the machete above my head
Disappointed when you don't
Because my music is my blood
If I'm not in pain,
I cannot sing
If you don't leave me bloody,
I cannot write
Light slits riddle my sight
So I won't put up a fight
Leave my body as a crooked map
So you can retrace my steps on my corpse
I suffer for your name
So drain me
Death prophetic

We are the shattered children of this Broken World
Tormented by memories of past lives
Standing on Mount Sinai
Beholding a valley of Shadows
Thou art with me
Search for Salvation
Search for Him
Search for Her
Inside the wasted mind
We dine
Then become divine
A Last Supper
Jacob is the **Judas**
Turn wine to water
Then walk
Like a crucifix sphinx
As this system blinks
Three nails set us free
From schizophrenic slavery

451

I'm burning at 451 degrees Fahrenheit
Read or die through my sight
Blinded on a holocaust night
Kristallnacht
Street brother walked the wrong block
And got shot
Body shakin, Luciferian illumination
Holy Spirit crawling your spine
With a tingling sensation
What's a heathen redemption
Practitioner of ritual abortion
Murder coercion
We're Legion
So make sure you're fuckin' breathing
Cause revolution is in season
We're done with kneelin'
Shout it out if you're still feelin'
And reelin', spinnin', every layer peelin'
Revealing a light held back
Factions, looks like you seen a ghost
   when showed the facts

A new believer handed a religious tract
Revoke that suicide pact
React, don't hold back, you book of blood
I'll run across a landmine to prove it was a dud
So open up your pages
Red tattooed by sages restraining
The temptation to bomb Central Station
Cause I know the ragin' anticipation
To become the causation
For the annihilation
Of a corporation
So will we have damnation, creation,
    or reincarnation?
Create this a declaration of oration
Consider this a salutation
A letter from a social leper
They painted us as debtors
Invisible coins become the fetters
What's better than to send a beggar
To the shredder
Dehumanize your enemy
To a dirty monkey
Breathlessly and helplessly
An entity decaying mentally and physically
So readily accept the penalty for your ecstasy
This is how it's meant to be
The remedy for entropy
Is in your brain chemistry
Degrading a system
So how can we gain wisdom
When we're hard-wired to
    electric fire

And our only desire is to acquire?
Mechanical Animals
Saturated with tailor-made pathogens
Rotted out with a plastic abdomen
Haunted by binary phantoms
Reminding you you'll die with a
    memorandum
Black balled, the Shack called, the track stalled

Leaving me silent
Anticipating the violent
We must be fluent in our movement
The inducement of improvement
So vent your dissent
Till the foundations have been bent
And you know you're heaven sent

See Media

CNN slices and kills my face
    Instilling fear
And void of any trace of logic
    Or ingrained with sympathy
For the people that it speaks to
    Empathy is absent
And for now we See Media
    As somewhat of a necessity of Arcadia
But arcane
    And understood only by a few
We knew nothing as we're attacked
    On every front by ads and stacked fliers
To buy shit we never needed
    But this is a warning that goes unheeded
We've been implored and entreated
    And challenged to go for two days
With no media
    But unbalanced goes the weasel
And down down goes the eyelids
    With nothing to watch
We can't run away from ourselves

  Don't leave me alone with my thoughts
They're just empty shelves

See Media
See Media
See Media

With nothing but reality TV to watch
  We're left to die
As intelligence is botched
  And communist stations make us subservient
Docile and ignorant
  Searching for a way to prevent
The constant dulling of our minds
  Unbind from the machine that's unkind
To our growth of consciousness
  And remind us that we're sheep
Ready to be raped and dissected
  Because we agreed to it
And willingly became infected
  By the media tyrants
Brainwash air giants
  And sin spinners
Let us die or be free into the atmosphere
  Let me be a bringer of truth
To audiences not prepared
  LISTEN
But I'm no singer
  I'M A KILLER
Your minds are what I aim for
  Your lives are what I strive for
Through observation I became sore

    Same form
Color chloroform onto vacant eyelids
    They can't see me
Till television stations
    Buy kids...

See Media
See Media
See Media

Crack open the lens
    And see what cums out
Pus pouch
    I see it bleed raw footage
And shout out
    For substance more than what is given
Images void of thought
    Corporations driven
By nothing beyond money
    Life isn't sunny
And this ain't funny
    There remains a drought of
Conscious decision-making
    Come watch us
As we sit in front of the god-box
    For eternity
As the infinite locks us into our chairs
    Making us stare into the void
But you don't care
    About the children of the empty laugh...
Metal clap resonates art with no craft

KILL YOUR GOD
KILL YOUR GOD
KILL YOUR...

                  TV!!!!!!!!

I'm screaming for you
        But you still don't see me...

See Media...
See Media...
See Media...

Jiz and Rainbows

You are *Rainbow Brite*
And I am *David the Gnome*
And I still remember all the cartoons
I'd watch at home
When I was six-years-old
Back from kindergarten
No,
I'm not like you
Watching *Power Rangers* or *Beetle Borgs*
Shit,
I'm *Stranger than Fiction*
I sunk my mind into *Care Bears*
And silky chairs
Watching *Muppet Babies*
That shit made my dreams cum true
Like *Lamb Chop* on my plate
And *Mister Rogers* staying up late
Watching four or five hours of shows...

Nickelodeon?
Forget *Blues Clues*

I watched *Rupert*
That weird little white bear in shoes
Give me old school cartoons like
Felix the Cat
Not some violent Asian shit
That shit is whack
What?
You telling me *The Neverending Story* is gay?
Put that shit away
I can't stand your hateful honesty
Cause you were jerkin' off to *Adventures in Odyssey*

Ummm...fuck it
This poem ain't flowin'
The way that I wanted it to
Cause whenever I try to be funny
It doesn't work
And deep down I'm imagining
Rainbow Brite getting fucked by *Felix the Cat*
And the *Care Bears* dousing the audience
With their love juice
Yeah...that's where it goes
And it flows all down your leg
And when you beg for the show
To be over,
I'm watchin' *Ducktales*
And countin' clovers

Alice

When I was a baby,
    I was born through the looking glass
What it is, it wouldn't be and I sink into the grass
I looked up at the sky and dreamt of the Land of Wonder
Falling through the glass, my world was torn asunder
I thought I was Lewis Carroll, but I am really Alice
Remembering the field they took me to, I'm feeling the malice
Because they raped me again and again and flashed their cameras
Clouds flash, time-lapse,
    and white knights help me forget about the love
Eat me, Drink me,
    adapting to where I need to go, I'm grabbing the gloves
But the fan makes me shrink to the size of a child
I've become the little girl, written my fate and styled
The experience to that of a trip
Sip, sip this and lick the tip
Of the tea cup that flies with the butter
He stuttered, and I was his dream child
And being a pornographer could make him seem wild
But I understand this and what he was about
I love him nonetheless, so there's no need to shout

I just wish to kiss the Mad Hatter
The curiouser and curiouser doesn't really matter
Since the March Hare be my pet
Chess set is my home but I'm caught in the net
Of hookah, dreams, and caterpillar lies
Time sighs in the dust, forget all my tries
To educate the Tweedles, it just seems unwise
To outrun the Jabberwocky on his own terrain
I'll lead it to the Queen cause she's become a pain
In my face, this isn't a race to the other side of the board
But if you play by the rules,
     there's *No Exit* of your own accord

Daddy,
     do you remember when I wore that yellow dress for you?
It is true that you hated me,
     baited me, created me from all that's new
Come true, my dreams, please,
     I beg you for hallucinations
Sensations up my spine and remind me of a world of situations
Distractions from a life unlived, revived and contrived
From stories dug up from long ago
You wrote me, these are the seeds that I sow
And now and then
     I'll still be your little girl
Throw me down the rabbit hole
     and let the colors swirl

Hellion

I run off God's own ethanol
A stench with gall
So who's got the ball
And who's court is this
Which elite can I dis
Dismiss it with a fist
Oh, I insist
That you finally enlist
In the army
That'll help us coexist
But I missed the sign-up sheet
Cause she couldn't be discreet
And I lost my hand within the sheets
So I was unable to write
Even to utter my name at night
The pencil picked a fight
Between the lines hidden from sight
Is it strength to show our might
But that doesn't make it right
I'm riding that beam of light
It doesn't touch the sun

It's just a rainbow for fun
Words that'll never be outdone

Word
Who's the leader of this herd?
Is a phoenix a spirit or a bird?
A question so absurd
I wouldn't expect it to be fulfilled more
I write above blood and gore
So much more than a seeping sore
Bleeding on the floor
With cuts, I'm loosing breath
Inching toward my death
Shadows bring the Thoth
Foaming mouth full of froth
Like the head of a beer
LSD to see clear
Listen, can you hear
A suicide of peers
You lack empathetic tears
At the River's Edge
We built a callous hedge
To hear a killer bragging
So I'm lagging behind
Any feeling for the body that we find
This flesh is just rind
To slice our own kind
Inside, defined pulp
Like a blood orange
   step back and gulp
Behold your Wizard of Gore
You're begging for more

Simon Says to sever the core
Dead bodies melted down to Iron Ore
Drop Dead Sexy
Lifeless like Ellie
Hellion
What Is It? we sellin' 'em

PART FIVE

The Bondage of My Madness Loosening

Elemental Junkie

[Air]
Ingest me like a chemical compound
I'm here to shatter ground and astound
But if my head could ever quit its pounding,
I could do with a little grounding
Cause my place is in space
Floating above an atomic rock,
I love God's creation,
    but we put it on lock
So I take a hammer to this clock
Crystal shards
To get cosmic lawyers disbarred
But give some regard
    to what we discard
Inhale like a whale
And become eco-avant-garde
Here's a charge to be on guard
When we discover the Alchemy of Air
Send a prayer to heaven
So ignorance can't ensnare our brethren
Give progression some discretion

Cause when our dreams were torn asunder,
They thought bread would quell our hunger
But fertilization
   for a temporary solution
Left the future generation
With a legacy of pollution
Through nitrogen destruction
We may have greater production
But it comes at the cost of natural disruption
There will be regulation
So take care with my air
Because no breath
   is our death

[Earth]
I descend to the land
   like rain
Barefoot on oil-slicked sand
   I feel its pain
This is a chain of events
That will lead to our descent
Unless we prevent the extent
To which we circumvent the balance
For man, that's the real challenge
So I cry,
   looking up at my sky
We think life is about a fancy yacht
Or what we've bought
But I ask you now:
   What's the molecular makeup of my dripping snot?
Buck shot forming out of Astral Ash

Take your monatomic gold
   and trade it in for cash
I'm bleeding hurricanes from a gash
And I wouldn't bother to
   lick your blood from the grass
Puff puff pass
And pass out
Don't look down
Cause then you'll hear a deafening sound
That'll drown out His voice
This has always been a choice
So I choose to rejoice
   with an active voice
This is our planet
So let's try to understand it
What happens if our habits wreak havoc?
Food riots and savage madness
   irreversible damage
So much waste
   Maybe we've become the garbage
We are part of this Earth
   Let's not become Her curse

[Fire]
If we cleanse, my friends
Let's look at the problem through this lens
Our forests are burning
   but our consciousness is turning
We're aching for some learning
And we pray to be discerning
Psyches start your churning

Think,
    maybe returning to an earlier state
Death won't be our fate
Don't sedate, we need to update
If your soul is ablaze,
    you can't afford all these delays
So many ways to raise awareness
About a home that we all cherish
But if we're garish,
    then we perish
I wish that we could flourish
Only if we could nourish
    Physical, Spiritual, Mental
I'm a Junkie Elemental
Fire mixed with Ice
    we may be detrimental
My heat of desire,
    tempted to be judgmental
I must remember to be gentle
Water can still burn
If the thorn is spilling oil
Tied to the stake and lit
    Screaming for our mortal coil
Charred, there's ashes in the soil
I bleed
But all we really need
Air, Earth, Fire, Water
So why then do we slaughter
Each other and destroy our Mother
We made Gaia a liar
And set her on fire
It's no surprise we're headed for the funeral pyre

So I choose to hoist
A moist tongue above a host
Speaking with the Holy Ghost
She's the one I feel the most
I'm burning like a roast
And standing at the coast
A breeze felt with ease

[Water]
No more hailing tears
I want the music of the spheres
To me it's finally clear
Negativity will never set us free
So this is a decree
    to search for symmetry
We'll never all agree
There's a degree of ambivalence
Sometimes I feel like
    a cut tree or a dead sea
But striving for equality,
    individuality, and equilibrium
We're in need of a baptism
We killed the fish,
    so now we want Aquarius
Surrounded by the blue,
    but most of it is poisonous
So float with us
But we're splitting like a delta
And creating Helter Skelter
I'm a child of the water

But we're in a schizophrenic schism
    far from peace
Like the polytheistic gods of Greece
I'm at least under the belly of the Beast
I see its Marks
It ain't a myth or a farce
It's all so dark
I feel like a little boy left in a park
In need of Captain Planet
Cause I'm famished
Waste is rampant
We landed
In a beautiful Oasis
    but still act like we're all stranded
Granted, so now I light a candle
As humans, we're like a virus
We strangle, hack, and mangle
Everything has already been created
So we think of ways to desecrate it
What we decided is not painless
My spirit is the waves of the river
    and I shiver
Quiver
Some day we will deliver
Hopefully not a society like The Giver
Let's make the world less bitter
Never let it whither
Transcend is what we must
Bring light and resurrection
To this nightmare opium den
So pardon our dust,
    The systematic rust

Passed down through years of lust
I feel the manic gusts
As this frigid panic thrusts
Our epidemic must
Find a soluble end
Through visions we contend
Our soiled souls we mend
I hope the healing ain't pretend

Now let's repair the planet
   And this time,
      Let's fuckin mean it

Join Hands in the Sands

I am the sun, the moon, the stars
    and the bars
And as our hearts slowly become one
    I won't be as hard
I shall become softer
    like fluid waves of cotton
That ebb and flow into one continuous sea
    Rockin to the beat of the sun
I am not the drum
    I am the gun
That slings semen
    and sends women on the run
I sink into the bed
    I'm red
And I become the bed
    Not able to wake
I continually shake
    the barbed wire and lead bullets
That pierce my spirit
    They're tracing like fluid
Into the Milky Way

Beyond the Milky Way
Beyond what I say
    For now I lay you down to sleep
But the journey untethered or weathered
    Even though my clothes be tattered
My soul hasn't shattered
    I bleed you
I feed you
    I need you
And as if that hadn't mattered
    You leave me to rot and to write
And to fight against Jesus
    My tongue suffers suffocated
As I scream he fails to heed us
    And this must
Hate must
    And will rust the world away
Unless we douse it with our hearts
    Our conscious love for a day
And finally say WOW
    What the fuck have we done to ourselves?
Then I delve into what I still don't fully understand
    But I can stand up and recite
The words I write at night by lamp light
    And it will be a sight to behold
For we are all on this journey of
    mind, soul, body, life, death, grief, happiness, success,
failure, suicide, life support, euthanasia, sensation,
redemption, condemnation, openness, and closure
    But bring me closer to assimilation
Into the collective river which is us
    Our conscious spirit that opens to the sky

I will never die
>   So help me try to combat what's become
>   destructive in time
And even though I hurt
>   And am crooked of spine
We must join hands in the sands
>   and heal this world that's unkind

Have I come full circle again?
But a circle is never full till it is joined
By every person who has lived, is living, and will live
And you may ask me,
Jacob, is that possible?
To which I reply,
Of course, the circle is already drawn in the sand
All that is left to do is step into it
And taking your hand I lead every person into the future
Into the unknown
To face the orange balls of ice
That rain into the atmosphere
They've become the projectiles
The walnuts to the dome
But who's the enemy if the whole world is my home?
My enemies are the ones who take no side
The ones we know have something to hide
So much has become tainted and corrupted
I fought against not fighting and my spirit has erupted
And conducted the lightning made of one thought
I caught it
Spun out to space in haste

Without knowing the substance of what was given to me
It's easy for you to see
You who already know what it was
A challenge to make it grow
And not to wither
Come hither, my child
And speak with the wild
For you have been there
Grown out your hair
And sputtered back onto the track
Toward rebirth, recreation, temptation,
Sensation, creation, deception, but rejection of destruction
Realization to the point where you cease to destroy all you love
And tear down only when necessary
But to create without holding back
You are my God, child, meditate with me this day
And we just may become one body
So please be my eyes, my ears, my voice
And lead my people back to the circle
The river, the wind, the spirit, the infinite
And you will be their Ankh
Leading the battle of the mind
Pick up your pens, my friends
Cut the binds
And burn the blinds
From off of your eyes

I am Raging War

B-CUM

Suffer all that hasn't become everything. Walk it and meet up with the energy of the ones you are supposed to commune with. B-CUM me. B-CUM you. B-CUM black. B-CUM white. I am every color. Become my concubine and we will have sex over the page. I will cut my wrists and bleed these verses. Please menstruate onto my word and I will love you always. Cupping my hands, I shall drink of your river. Bless me with your curse and I shall B-CUM it. B-CUM the mantra. B-CUM. B-CUM. B-CUM. B-CUM. B-CUM. B-CUM. B-CUM. B-CUM. But does anything B-CUM or are we already what we will always be? I shall be your cum. Your flow. Your wetness. Baptize me henceforth in femininity. Have me worship you and bleed into and out of your vagina. Make me into that being of light that radiates energy, sexuality, and wisdom. For cumming together may still be able to open portals into the stars. We are the everything. Plants be our feet, suns be our heads, cough and bring into being. And it has been created out of nothingness. Out of my mind. Out of all that was, is, and will be. And it is I. I have not B-CUM. I am. I have not B-CUM. I am. I have not B-CUM. I am. I have not B-CUM. I am.

Psychedelic Fragments

MKULTRA broke us down into Psychedelic Fragments
Within the balance of the Dragon
Her magnet attracted my planets
In segments, she mirrored my talent with enchantment
I inscribed the parchment
With every incantation
Every invocation
All divination
Ecstatic gnostic stimulation
My grid of occult organizations
The Crowley Illuminist
Satanist Christ
Pan harnesses the Zeitgeist to be sacrificed
I take master genes to splice
Listen to the whisper entice
As I become Priest Poltergeist
Paradise is the Bride Price
Through days and endless nights
I take you to these heights

You busted me apart

A devastated shattered blackened heart
Give birth to the magician
Self micro fission
It's my mission to listen to confessions of Christians
We're shamans institutionalized
Sterilized
Sanitized
Lucifer ritualized
I am Jesus in Bohemian Grove
I am the tea on your stove
The DMT deep in the cloves
You are so very close
To when the Kundalini arose
The path we chose
As we meditated in corpse pose
All 18,000 worlds froze
Intro a crystalline structure
My Monarch Butterfly flutters
As I remove all the mental clutter
We're on an Island of Shutters
My Inner Child is Butters

Now!

Wake up from your programming
The Matrix human farming
Pan causes Panic that's alarming
My honesty disarming
We embody the singularity
A Luciferian music industry
Let's choose to experience this differently
Still a bit immorally

For the Devil there is sympathy
A symphony of imagery
In pieces we're easier to handle
I own vagabond sandals
And the palms of a vandal
Orchestrating scandal
Any place I dangle
When the sun and moon unite
Let the phoenix flight into the night
Every flame and every sight

She picks up the pieces of my skull
The bones are a bit grey and dull
Become whole, your own handler
Schizophrenic Messianic tongue channeler
I'm on a level of Avatar
Technically I'm the Devil
Are you on my Level?
Together we cause upheaval
Mischievous, not evil
Like a curious weasel
I AM your handler
With an open vessel
No, wait, maybe you are mine
Nonetheless, you are Divine
Our union lets us climb
You must take my hand when I go blind
Grasp in the Dark
What is this we find?
How to be kind
Chill, and unwind
When we're bound too tight

There's no peace, just against everything we fight
But really, we're against ourselves tonight
Thinking of 'ifs' 'whys' or 'mights'
Pan will erase your fear of flight
You're mistaking excitation for fright
I AM your programmer
And your deprogrammer
How could I liberate
Before I dictate
If you listen, I'll extrapolate
It's only to you I masturbate
The Earth's crust begins to shake and vibrate
What if I had the antichrist price on your head
We're all already dead
Just waiting for the flesh to shed
If we're just waiting to go home
You miss all the fun of passing through the Zone
I clone you
Bone you
Fuck the original you to make it True
Here, I'm handing you the clues
To figure out NOW what's new
Yeah, I've had companions, a few
But with this one, it's beyond thought
I just know
That for everything I've fought
I maintain a bright auric glow
The Never-ending flow
Straight from the Naad, I strobe
Stroke
Watch you inside my snow globe

We're fractured in the same places
But we remain whole throughout our stasis
Easier to control the faceless
The homeless
Not if you're a Temptress
The Mambo Priestess
In a past life I would have bathed in blood
Drank a semen flood
Ate the entrails of fetuses
Still I dream of severed penises
I'm a scorpion for a reason
Now it's sowing season
And I'm grateful
To have more than a plateful
God is beautiful
Even Satan cums to Jesus
Do you choose
Since there's no game to lose
I have both Yeshua and Lucifer close within my heart
So I remain a work of Art
Lucifer is now returned to God's side
Back to the start
Flipping outside and inside
Let's make this a better ride
I had my fun on the inside
Got tired of Satanic Ritual Abuse
So I took a snooze
Now I'm awake
And know Creation is at stake
Now, right now, I command
Your DNA to activate
Now you must teach the world to facilitate this liberation

Utopia is not just imagination
It's a possible future projection
Not the antichrist kingdom
I am a singular dot grown to phallic symbolism
Psychic vampirism
What's happening?
The fappening
I am the sexual energy building
The Guru of GodFuck, fuck it
If it works, suck it
I tuck it back to stealth a dyke
Could've gotten a Master's in Psych
When you realize you're a sleeper cell, like
CIA brain, not insane, Central Intelligence Lane
Perfect Illusion of Fame…

Thank You

The blackout we know it
This is a lot hotter than we anticipated
But grab your sunglasses
When we wake up on fire
Fire and rain cleanse
Water to flow
Fire to heat our spirit
Fill with your reclaimed power
Really Power to the People
Is THIS
This principle of longing for unity
Why did you torture yourselves with the opposite
Before you could see we are ONE?
I am not the one with the answers
You must formulate those yourself
In free verse
Rhyme has it's place
Life is more a free flow
A free style
If you will
A tantric ballet

A dance with your God
For Eternity
The difference between dance
And Fear
Is translation
We have become lost in translation
Google babble?
Dabble in black magic?
Talking through the static
We see beneath
As you hide in plain sight
You fuck yourselves
Blood orgy obsessed
There's a specific time to undress
I told you:
I signed under duress
You didn't guess?
GOD BLESS

I Am One of Them, I Am All of Them

I am continually dying among the living
And I find myself living among the dead
However, my mother is among the living
And my father is amongst the dead
And then there comes me
The one who doesn't belong, you see
So I scream in silence
As the violence of unridden hooves
Pummel my body with their noise
Swimming in the sediment
I wait
For the sky to accept the girls
And boys that I have made love to
What is to come?
What is to come for me?
What is to come for you?
And what is to come for all of us?
For we are all of the same spirit
As we remain prisoners of the never-ending

Crimson pendulum
That pulled from the cave of ba-dum dum dum
I'm still feeling the ripples of the bomb
Ba-dum dum dum
Please, I beg you to stretch your hand
Out to suddenly connect with the electricity
Pulsing from my palm
Where has this power come from
Pour the soul into me from the sun
And the galaxies of every hand I've ever touched
And every hand that's ever touched me
Push my hair back to reveal a hidden door
To my mind
Open that door so the tails of iguanas
Can air themselves and combine with the thoughts
That are brought forth from my sleeping fortifications
Motherfuckers need to look into my eyes
So as to share my hallucinations
That come not from drugs
But from the goddesses, the gods, the heart,
The spirit, the love the hate, the words, the humans,
The subhumans, the superhumans, the mortals,
And the immortals

I am one of them
I am all of them

PART SIX

Break Every Chain

Gettin Paid

This is a rhyme about
Gettin' paid, gettin' paid

You are my muse, my spirit
And you've made me rich beyond reason
Because you've spit these colors into
My eyes
Making my retinas shatter
And my pupils dilate
In order to make a larger whole
For your soul

Catch me if you can
But this ain't a race
And you're not a rabbit
I remember when they used to call me
Turtle
But now,
I can stand up straight
Since the vertebrae be fused
To the titanium of my soul

And I can drum out a
Bum bum bum
On the sticks, the clams, the snakes
That feather this expanse
Of unweathered talk
Of unspooned words
Of tortured wings
That will fall off once the sky
Becomes the color of wine

And I know
That you all know
That I know
That you know
I am not you
But in that fact I am
Becoming Everything
And that makes us the same

Part the ways
We are the parts of the world
And we are One
We are the sun
The fire, the living
And everything I have said here tonight
Will take flight into the darkest
And most narrow tunnels
That lead out of the spheres
Into another tunnel

And into you

My spirit
My guide
My myself
Because you are me
And I am you
And that is a picture of me
Even though it was developed as you
It bears my face

The constellationness of time conflagrations
Because the sky is aflame with airwaves
That ripple with our voices

I still exist to grow roots in cosmopolitan gardens
To sprout no thought
Just phallic symbols
But I grab them and jerk them
Till they spurt—
Blood

Because I know they just exist here
To transform into vaginal imagery
My muse
My spirit
You've made me rich beyond reason
Because even though I can't have children
You aid me in giving birth
And for this I thank you

This shit ain't about
Gettin' paid, gettin' paid

And this shit
Does not
Rhyme

Break Every Chain

Rage war in heaven
Rage war on earth
Show me the stars, galaxies,
Violent explosions of spirit
And if I don't return,
I have committed my soul as a soldier
And succumb to Eternity

We are artists
And when we travel,
It's a gift to every person in the world

This is for everyone who was ever called a faggot
     when they had the balls to be themselves!

This is for everyone who was told to shut the fuck up
     when they chose to speak instead of be silent!

This is for everyone who was pushed back down
     after they chose to stand up!

This is for everyone with an opinion
>   different than the majority!

This is for that kid who refuses to conform or transform
>   into that "typical public school kid"!

This is for every child who was ever raped,
>   but felt that it would be better to make light of it!

This is for you!
The ones who struggle!
The ones who feel they have no voice!
You do!
All you need to do is
>   SPEAK WITH IT!

We are the Forevers of this land
But what if there comes a time
>   when I have nothing left to give you?
Will you come and claim my heart?
My Scepter?
However, I now know that I am
>   part of this war
This somewhat silly war of clashing egos
But there are the important battles
>   that are necessary to fight
And so I gladly take up my sword
>   to cut the established to ribbons
The problem is that you don't know
>   where you are going
You aren't ready to be part of the
>   meeting of the spirits

By what means shall we arrive at this meeting place?

Shall it be by train?
By bus?
By car?
By bike?
Or shall it be by our own feet
    quietly pattering the road leading to the gates?
Or by our words?
Our voices uttering the songs
    of our lives
To become kin to whomever else
    is listening
To whomever has eyes to hear it
And ears to see it

And since we find ourselves on a Duality planet
We must break every chain tethering us to extremes
Follow me into the circle of the Ouroboros
As our Kundalini pulls our souls from the cycle
Lay down hate and learn to Love again
So we may seize the day
Harness the Power of Now
To end a spiritual war
That has lasted for far too long

The embodiment of the And Consciousness
Within the Middle Way
The spine as pillar of neutrality
Leading to this meeting of the spirits
So we may unite once again

Not to fight a senseless war
But to witness the fact the enemy is us
So love thy enemy as thyself
And realize the mirror has turned within
To illuminate your own darkness
To love your Shadow
Is to break its chain

As the Dark Tethers rupture
And the whole system is torn asunder
We look to God for guidance
We look to our connection to our higher self
We pray
And finally see the God in the Mirror
Looking back at us from ourselves
In solidifying cloud forms
Claim your sovereignty
And break every chain

Cloud Atlas

We've spanned a billion lifetimes
To court each other's spirit
We seduce hearts
And pluck the strings of longing
Conducting concertos of epic romances
Blossoming in the spring
Me and she
We always sing

As I look for atlases in the clouds,
I remember I can't read maps
The territory seems fluid
To swim into its rapids seems treacherous
But we press on through time and space
Pan-dimensionally probing every incarnation
The loving way
That meditation tingles the imagination

The layer of film stretches and bursts
Skin on skin as we conceive
What and in whom do we believe

I went so far I couldn't even dream
On the gray edges of the hologram
I took the holy sacrament
Melded with the one within the Matrix
The Architect of my Buddhist design
But they can't catch me for committing
A thought crime

As me and she stray,
We converge
Not realizing the fusion
The androgynous metamorphosis
Written in code in hieroglyphics
We connect to the Field
The joy of the mystics
Lifetime after lifetime within the lighthouse of the super mind
We've been the collective and the individual
Shape-shifting, a holistic actor playing every part
She comes and shines her part upon the stage
And I am there
With her always from Age to Age

We span bio-rhythms
—me and her—
We encapsulate supernovas
—me and her—
We are Mount Vesuvius
—me and her—
We are an ecosystem

Me and her

Me and her
I swear the planetary time warp
Collects souls of our departed
The complex web we've weaved
Trapped our essence within it
But we distill
From millennia to millennia
Crystallizing
The alchemist purifying his gold
If we individuate at this rate
Breathe
We let our souls irradiate

I hear the *Cloud Atlas* play in my head
A symphony of loves and longing
Down through forever
We play the endless ballad
Without words
Our lives bleeding into the melody
From song to song, a different identity
So we play our part
We play our instrument
Take our seats and redistribute
Circling as the record does eternally
From birth to the hearse
That's life
Always ready to add a verse

Spiral of Infinite Space Encompassing

Stillness speaks
Through silent presence
You feel yourself as limitless
Suddenly you dissolve into the formless
And become the Expanse
Stars, galaxies, and infinite worlds
Are birthed and die within your Being

The spiral of infinite space encompassing
When you disappear into the void—a vacuum
The All becomes a vortex of no-thing
Within the no-mind all happenings of infinity
Exist in Eternity
And are the Emptiness
Yet the Time-Space continuum
Is squirted out of this
Like cosmic ejaculate
As we lick the goddess's yoni
Our cum B-CUMs the Milky Way

Earth is my orgasm
The Unmanifested transforms into a phantasmagoria

As Above So Below
As Within So Without
The macrocosm takes place within the microcosm
Feel the planets orbit inside your body
There is no God outside of you
You created this entire world
For yourself to explore
In that still voice you can hear it
Beyond the Spirit
This poem—you wrote it
It doesn't exist anywhere except inside you
All of these words—you are the author
Yours is the only cosmic signature
All of Life happens for you
And you Alone
The good, the bad, and the ugly
Are all servants of your evolution of consciousness
There is no Other

One Creator Creation

Ek Ong Kar
One Creator Creation
There is no separation
Between the form and the formless
Are one country
One domain
Where the Light of the World
Shines through
And becomes a lighthouse
For the boats traveling to the other shore
Breathing prana through every pore
Reach the limit to reach the core

There is no Creator
God *is* and God *is not*
The mystic speaks in paradox
In koans
In riddles
Because the experience of inner Beingness
Can only be pointed to
It cannot be expressed in words

They fall short
Poetry can reach far
But not the whole way
The poet is on his way to becoming a mystic
Truth is beyond the intellect
And to surrender
Is the absorption into the Ultimate Reality
Which is *you*—beyond the Beyond

As you travel from Here to Here
You could stay and rest in the Lotus Paradise
Rest, relaxation, enjoying the beauty of Life
Or *be* peace—and continue on *in* peace
Beyond Enlightenment there is more
Beyond Immortality there is more
Beyond the Beyond there *is*
Discover this in all its Glory
In the state of intense Grace
Beyond the Creation
Beyond the Creator
To the place where both are One
You push on to where the One
Becomes *Zero*
Silence
Voidness

Shunyata

The One Alone

Within the Black Void Silence of Space
I am the One Alone
I am the movement of Spirit
To create within the Nothingness
The Emptiness
Pure Mind—No-Mind
Even to use the word "I" is impotent
Purely am-ness
Beingness
At the center of our pure essence
Wherever beings exist
That's you coming into being
Truly beyond the duality
Beyond the beyond
Beyond enlightenment
Never reaching the end of Infinity is beautiful
For the dance lasts forever
The heart always overflowing with Love
To love is to be alone
Feeling All as a manifestation of the One
Which is you

God is the end
Not the beginning
In the beginning there is you
In the middle there is you
In the end there is you—and you are God
And truly there is no end
There is no beginning
You have always been
I have always been
We have always been
The pure bliss of emptiness
To connect to the Still Presence in the Now
Is to tap Eternity
I Am That I Am

PART SEVEN

Deathless We Live Infinitely

Alchemy

From the book "Jung: A Journey of Transformation" by Vivianne Crowley

alchemy (Note from the author: the EMPHASIS is my own)

Jung's GRAIL DREAM in India led him to reexamine the Western esoteric tradition of ALCHEMY with the insights he had gained from the WISDOM of the EAST. Yoga TRANSFORMS the BODY, MIND, and SPIRIT; alchemy is ostensibly about CHANGING BASE metal to GOLD, but Jung believed the outer operation was simply a METAPHOR for a more profound INNER CHANGE. He realized that alchemy was not just an early scientific and technical process. It involved an elaborate COSMOLOGY in which the HUMAN BEING, the microcosm, was a REFLECTION of the COSMOS, the macrocosm. Since macrocosm and microcosm reflect one another, by engaging in the TRANSFORMATION OF MATTER, the alchemists would at the same time TRANSFORM THEIR OWN CONSCIOUSNESS. Jung believed that the alchemists were projecting onto matter their own psychic processes. Some were aware of the deeper SYMBOLIC meaning, but many were not.

However, the preparations involved in alchemical work hint at the SPIRITUAL discipline involved. Practitioners had to be in a state of spiritual purity and had to renounce all covetousness. The attitude was to be one of DETACHMENT and COMPASSION, and the work accompanied by PRAYER.

Jung found that many of his patients who were undergoing inner changes on their journey of INDIVIDUATION had dreams that resembled the processes described in alchemy. For him, the stages of alchemy became a sophisticated symbol system that represented the ARCHETYPES of the COLLECTIVE UNCONSCIOUS and the different stages of the individuation process.

The physical process involves a series of scientific operations using furnaces of varying temperatures, stills, flasks, and the alchemist's miraculous spherical vessel. As the base metal in their scientific apparatus DIVIDED into MALE and FEMALE elements and THEN REUNITED again to a NEW and PRECIOUS SUBSTANCE that contained BOTH MALE AND FEMALE, so too did the alchemists' SOULS.

Crucified on a Ten Strip

Shout out to the Deadhead OG
I found my vein and injected that K-Rino flow
God help me spin this Merkabah
And spit it infected with a Drunvalo glow
Let's go!

Thoth, Hermes, Mercury
I'm Thrice Great
Like the Trinity in a city full of heartache
I am that which you will become
From street bum to front of the auditorium
My cranium is meddlesome
The system is a crematorium
I live in a martyrdom gymnasium
They want to lock me away in a sanitarium
Cause I'm scum
I close my eyes and hum
Remember where I'm from
This physical life is a medium between
The maximum and minimum
Student of a Divine Curriculum

Dream
I imagine when I go platinum
I'll feel like I've been drinkin' opium

Yeah, I rolled up to the spot
The 420 lot
Here to see the Whodathunkit show
It's my birthday and I don't know who knows
They don't know I'm about to blow
Find yo Buffalo Mind State
Imagine carrying Domino as an embryo
Oblivious and Indigo
Got aborted
She desecrate
I embody Pan and Socrates prophecies
Consummate with me
Then contemplate how I fascinate, educate, and elevate
With communication assassination

I don't even gotta be trippin' to write this
Blow me one last kiss and I'll diss your setlist
In a semi-opaque lyric mist
Alice delivered me from an eternal Tryst
Brought me back to the hologram to speak the the fam
So aim that cam
Did I mention the beautiful trans-girl I met at Ray's
She entered like a Luna moon ray
Sailor Mercury lollipop fantasy
Maybe she'll be taken by my Mastery
Vivid Monet Dadaist painted imagery
Maybe she favors me
Cause my relationship's a triangle

Come to my Scorpion web and be entangled

Before the show I ate three mushroom chocolates
With opioids and cannabis
Examine this cancerous dangerous tantalus — vision
A nebulous nautilus — incision
Ravenous for the scandalous and prosperous — television
So make sure you bring some provisions

Back to the journey
My rap story
Study me in your laboratory
Till you find a category
The stage is my territory
I proved it
Go view it
Fuck it!
Around the campfire fed Stefinitely some mushrooms
To peer through the gloom
Like K I'm already outta space like a crowded room
I felt my double heart start to beat in unison
Watching the stage, my friends set up their instruments
I'm getting visuals
The moment is critical
Realize the cyclical
Grim fed me molly from his palm
And left DMT in my van for another adventure
Which piece of experience will I capture?

Whodathunkit starts playing
We three assume the position of the Trinity
Stefinitely, Annie, me

Synchronicity, feel me
So I synchronized the energy with both sides of the pyramid
When it came time for this kid to do a gig
As if it was manifested was a Jitterbug Perfume
Don't ever assume that the pyramids are tombs
We are Pan chillin' in trees that always bloom
I own every eye in the room
So when I was called to spit a freestyle
I just smiled from the Nile and walked down the aisle

I got on the mic and stunned them
The audience and musicians jammin'
We're here to end the Spirit famine
I'll pause so these lyrics you can examine

I said, "I'm not like you
I came here to enlighten you
I'm just like you"
An alien from a Dark Nebula, Gypsy Jeweler
Alternate Egypt manufactured
Nilotic, Clive Barker and fractured
Till she was raptured
Integrated
I thought about it and masturbated
We are Pan: The ManWoman
David, just shut up
That's right, I'm just David talkin' on the microphone
Suddenly the tone switched chromosomes
And all I could see was this blinding light attaching
    to my backbone
All alone I had to cross this milestone
Then I'm surrounded by 7,000 angels

Who placed me in a manger and said I was in danger
That I was about to viscerally experience
	a dark informational system
But as a human, you're a bit like a piston
Your constant up and down keeps you going
But you need to transcend Duality and continue floating
You are part of Christ Consciousness rotating
We've been calling while you're down there debating
Quit narrating, and vacate
Earth so we can consolidate
Venus needs your passport
Terra wants you tied up in court
Jews want the money and the comfort
And to the cross they'll be your escort

What?

You've been Crucified On A Ten Strip
How's it feel to take that trip
I lost grip on reality, InI, and Identity
Literally, nailed to the cross
Still behind the mic
This is how I like it
So I don't fight it
When beneath me opens a vortex of sex
I looked in both my lovers eyes as I was pulled
	from the simple to the complex
As you go down it gets denser
Negative, a bit tenser
As I crossed over CocoRosie came to me
	in a single form — a fairy
She fluttered her wings and spoke to me:

"It has come time for you to know,
All you could ever want or be shown is in your very soul"
She was gone and I fought to be back Within the Light
This is the Well: hell dot com
The place for meth moms and discarded Uncle Toms
Trapped in the Deep Web it's for God's presence you beg
Cause in this place you've no use of either leg
Caught in the sticky sticky internet
Fallen in the trap of the intellect
Home of my demons and failed projects
I fear this is eternal torment
But I remember I'm God's informant
With positive thoughts to implant
If I won't transcend this negative netting
It's only cause I think I can't
Ohms and songs I chant
Grant me passage to the upper realms
With purpose of spreading this message

I rush to leave hell like John Constantine
We need God to intervene in this machine
Demons try to pull me down, but I get out clean
Like a Nazarene
Doused the obscene in gasoline
Kicked that habit off a ravine along with nicotine
But still in between like a mezzanine
So I dreamed of somewhere serene
Instantly I am in a field that is evergreen
This had not been foreseen but this is
     where the team was to reconvene
I walked up on a picnic of three beings
Rubbed my eyes cause I couldn't believe what I was seeing

Sitting sipping tea were Joshua, Krishna, and Siddhartha
I asked them, "Where is Hermes?"
Joshua said, "He's studying in the Halls of Amenti, he sent we to speak to thee"
Krishna gestured to me to join them on the blanket
Thank him
He handed me the tea and I drank it

"Now you are Pan, aren't you?" Said Siddhartha
"We heard you're a hiphoppa, stop us if we're wrong but we know some of your songs"
She spit my words back
Lyric for lyric of BiSolar's seventh track
They stopped
"You know you are Hip Hop," said Josh
"We don't want this Nilotic, she's a bit posh
Oh, my gosh, did I say that?"
He blushed
Krishna spoke once the wind had hushed
She looked at me, I looked a bit flushed
As my brain turned to mush
Siddhartha laughed and says,
"We're just fucking with your mind
You're really deaf, dumb, and blind
Took some drugs and are on a bad sidewind
Smoke some of this weed, it'll treat you kind"
I took a hit, turned, and what I saw made sense a bit
Life, even IF we can make sense of it
It's just you:
A fat old man with a rug
Meditating, no drugs
He smiles at you with e-hugs

I guess I'll go deeper, so I dug

When I turned back to the three
There were three beets before me
We are Pan, you can't ignore me
I have many stories
Some not as gory
Anyway, bout that get back to me

My heart suddenly hurt and I asked them why
"Why? Cause life is just a lie with an f in it
And death is definite
Sometimes you can't even measure it
You are dead, Pan, be grateful, treasure it"

"Your two hearts are stretching
Because your lovers will try to resurrect you"

Holy shit, wait, you knew?

Then Joshua spoke for the last time:
"We're here to show you the difference
Between resurrection and ascension"

They vanished
And as I passed through the Egg of Metamorphosis,
I realized what was constant in all this — is — David

I may not be from Tin Pan Alley
But I respect the artistry of my ancestry
My ability comes from my absurdity
My adversity turned to depravity then diplomacy

Embracing my deformity
I came to love all diversity

Like the CPU we are integrated
From the One these words dictated
My G card, I got the credential
The cutie twisted anarchist
Pan is the vocalist perfectionist
Who views it all as Providential

I'm under the surface
Can't feel my face
I'm breathin' ocean
Alive again, I get the notion
God has me up for promotion
She let me breathe again
I rush toward the shore with an explosion
It's December, I'm naked, it's winter
Blindly I call for Joshua's hand
I'm a Stranger in a Strangeland
Zero One man band
With no fans
Where are the Israelites, my clan?
I tried to find a tribe
But found only myself
A lone scribe
Now reopen the book you kept on your shelf
And transcribe all I describe

On the cross, before Josh expired
He wasn't even recognizable by his mum
I feel tired yet inspired

Experience the second cum
Third and forth
Respect East
Yahrushalem
Then face North
I bursted forth
Like a polar bear swim
Resurrection on a hymn, a wing, and a prayer
Teetering on the brim
Too slim with a million pseudonyms
Delirious
I asked for help and got a kick below the belt
Furious
Suddenly surrounded by police
I wished again for my heartbeats to cease — please
But all I got was increase
Till I was wrestled to the ground
Music is my sound
And this is my masterpiece
There was no peace and no release
They screamed at me: "What drugs are you on?"

Cocaine, PCP, meth, heroin, DMT, LSD,
Boomers, smack, nitrous, crack, angel dust
Soul and spirit rust

I was on none of the above
They shoved me in the ambulance, no love
Separated by the gloves
But out of the side of my eye I glimpsed a dove
Cuffed and zip-tied for the whole ride
I felt like I had died

Float as I glide
I woke up in a hospital, but still phenomenal
Unstoppable!
Me, an emcee, you think it's improbable
Fuck that, nothing is impossible
Breathe through my gills, I'm a beautiful fossil
MC Pan, the colossal apostle
Sent to jostle the docile
My heart is the strongest muscle
So I follow the light against all fright
I feel all right
I walk by faith cause of my inhibited sight
Into the corner room I go with the flow
I was a seed so long ago
Now I've grown
I sift through a bag of women's clothes
Slowly arose
And realized — I AM A WOMAN
God lifted the mental bans
Set me free to just me me
Lifted the agony of my blasphemy
And left me with the bravery
To withstand the conspiracy of the Agency
They'll never silence me
My Mercury harmony is fiery to the Industry
And the imagery of history lives on in infamy

I picked up the book on the table
Unplugged, the Matrix disabled
The title of the book enabled my label
It was "Jesus Calling"
No more stalling

This was the purpose of all my scrawling
Then I swear to God I heard trumpets
I declare this now: APOCALYPTIC IS TRIUMPHANT
I am called to the the Hierophant
In that moment I was awoken
For many are called but few are chosen

My breath came back
For a second I thought I was black
I'm a maniac having Sage flashbacks
Of *Clickety-Clack*
I'm a mic kleptomaniac
Opening my eyes I realized I'd been crucified then deified
I was resuscitated by Annie
The one with which I identified
My birthday had become surreal, mystified
So I took her to see if I could verify my sight for the butterflies
So I dosed her
She dosed me
For the revelation to occur
This gift was better than frankincense or myrrh
Let's be voyagers

We made Love
So much better than amateurs
Spirit is deeper than what you prefer
She held me like no one had before
She's the contributor to my Forevermore encore
Furthermore this is no metaphor
As we merged we connected to the Source
And I contemplated Power versus Force
Of course!

Electricity surged
As our energies converged
Her eyes closed as I studied her face
Immortally in the Space of Cosmic Grace
What concluded was the chase
She was every person of every race
We pull memory from a Universal Database
I saw the face of a saint
The face of a murderer
Women wearing war paint
Faces of healers and torturers
Faces of prisoners
And people of celebrated memoirs
Brothers and sisters
Maps to the Stars
Govindas and Siddharthas

"He saw the naked bodies of men and women, in postures and transports of passionate love. He saw corpses stretched out, still, cold, empty. He saw all these forms and faces in a thousand relationships to each other, all helping each other, loving, hating, destroying each other, and become newly born. Each of them was mortal, a passionate, painful example of all that was transitory. Yet none of them died, they only changed, were always reborn, continually had a new face. Only time stood between one face and another." — *Siddhartha*

"Are you about to cum?"
I opened my eyes and felt the opposite of numb
"Hold on," she said, "Or to the Ankh you will succumb
I'll initiate from behind or it will destroy and overcome you
The Metamorphosis, you made it too, picked up every clue
Made it True and made it through"

Then she touched the back of my neck with her fingers
Letting the tingles linger
She traced an Ankh with the glimmer of a thinker
I'm a vessel with which God likes to tinker
The Ankh combines and aligns with my spine
Connects one line between my Soul and Divine
So through me you can shine
Your blood is my wine
In the moment of climax
I feel the Universe with perfect syntax
Ankhing the sex energy
Pleasurably, an Osiris test
Never forget me, Death still brings us back nonetheless
Regained the Love I had denied
Anubis weighed my heart and I survived

Anubis weighed my heart
And I survived

Unified Horizon Line

The fabric of the blanket tapestry
Is drenched in effervescent rainbows
The eye can only see within this prism
As I project the organic
The machine orchestrates a synthetic frequency
We tune into this broadcast like a living radio
The brain waves of Living Light
Decipher this like a gelatin code
Beyond the ones and zeros is a figure
With her hand extended
Her heart open
Green beams leaking from the center of a star
As I dive into the principle of shimmering uncertainty
Her arms encircle the singularity trapped within my ribcage
With a rush of breath and water
The surface becomes a new landscape
Our unified soul is the horizon line

Something About Muffins

If there is ever a time you can't find me,
Don't worry
I'm doing all right
I've probably crawled inside a cave somewhere,
Counting my chakras,
Mumbling something about muffins
Wondering how many planes I can explore in a lifetime

See, I found my reason to live again:
Our children
And they have me giving birth
To moons I never knew I had
But I'm still struggling for the ability
To see the future
But I've decided to grow my hair
And I'll see this Terry on the other side

See he
Led me
To her
Jessica

She is my shining star
That burns in the heavens and will never go out
Because her light is immortal

See, at the beginning of Time there was Silence—then the Word
And the Word was with God
But now the Word is with me
And it is my duty to speak
Speak and it shall be created
The Nilotic took his own rib and created me,
Then I took one of my ribs to create her
Now my one rib less
Leaves me shape-less
Mind-less
And sex-less
I have made it so we are connected within the light
Now one plus one equals zero

Our bond is shattered but unbroken
We consummated our lust and now we commence
Toward the cosmos with every being we've ever known
This is our child
Our legacy
Now one plus one equals infinity
I know the math sounds strange,
And I seem to find myself aligning with divinity
But don't struggle,
Accept

I, I, and I am the holy trinity
And she is living proof that there is truth in immortality
We live as gods, regardless

And for whatever my task will be,
I shall carry the cross and crucify myself
And it will make them have more faith in me
I will hang from that cross,
They all will pierce my side with spears
And I will bleed the cosmos out of chaos

My body could die on that cross,
Bury me in a tomb and I would rise on the 7th hour
To speak in the 7th octave
And I would go toe-to-toe with Eternity
Until I was the savior of the human race
Well, maybe not the savior, but something
Cause I was definitely made for something
I cannot die
And some may question the love between Jessica and I
But it only makes me question them:

How have you saved the children?

For you must become like children to enter the Kingdom of Heaven

13

Frank Blue, Walter Fields, and Gary Bates were all in the park as I was told this fictional story.

Cell phone menu.

Some cell phones have call forwarding and you enter the number you want the calls forwarded to; the caller ID where you want the calls being sent.

Get all the creditors to call your cell phone and then put up a sign saying call this number (the number of the cell phone that's forwarded). When entering the number on the cell phone menu for forwarding, if they forward their calls to the State House, the phones will be ringing off the hook. And if they forward their calls to 911 or the non-emergency number. Like in the movie that's coming up that I am going to make. This is the script and Frank Blue is the hero, an Anonymous man in the park from Occupy Philadelphia.

If all the calls are forwarded to 911 in this movie, from all the Occupiers across the country on January 10th, there will be a widespread

911 overload where the government won't know if the calls are real or fake. They will send a car out for every call with an ambulance and fire truck. And the politicians will be forced to do something about the homeless.

From a man who loves his country, with a Braveheart, he stands up for the American Dream. He dresses like an Indian and throws the tea into the harbor. The calls are the tea in the Boston Harbor. Taxation without representation. He's just like John Wayne, Benjamin Franklin, Tim Horton, and Paul Revere. A Free and Accepted type man always on the Level with a Bible in one hand and a Compass in the other, not pulling the wool over anyone's eyes.

He travels West in search of Strength, East in search of Knowledge, and knows how to Pyramid an idea, but the end never comes because we live forever. The first death is the death of the Spirit; and our spirits are dying, but our endless faith that our deliverer has arrived has come to an end. Our flesh may perish, our second death, but our spirit lives on forever.

Avtar Simrit is a modern mystic and an artist. His writings and art are inspired by mystical inquiry as well as all inner and outer journeys. Avtar's main artistic mediums are the written word, Hip Hop music, and video. To check out his music and other work, visit the author's website: www.mc-pan.com.

www.ingramcontent.com/pod-product-compliance
Lightning Source LLC
Chambersburg PA
CBHW020906080526
44589CB00011B/468